Rethinking directions in language learning and teaching at university level

Edited by Barbara Loranc-Paszylk

Published by Research-publishing.net, a not-for-profit association
Voillans, France, info@research-publishing.net

© 2019 by Editors (collective work)
© 2019 by Authors (individual work)

Rethinking directions in language learning and teaching at university level
Edited by Barbara Loranc-Paszylk

Publication date: 2019/04/08

Rights: the whole volume is published under the Attribution-NonCommercial-NoDerivatives International (CC BY-NC-ND) licence; **individual articles may have a different licence**. Under the CC BY-NC-ND licence, the volume is freely available online (https://doi.org/10.14705/rpnet.2019.31.9782490057313) for anybody to read, download, copy, and redistribute provided that the author(s), editorial team, and publisher are properly cited. Commercial use and derivative works are, however, not permitted.

Disclaimer: Research-publishing.net does not take any responsibility for the content of the pages written by the authors of this book. The authors have recognised that the work described was not published before, or that it was not under consideration for publication elsewhere. While the information in this book is believed to be true and accurate on the date of its going to press, neither the editorial team nor the publisher can accept any legal responsibility for any errors or omissions. The publisher makes no warranty, expressed or implied, with respect to the material contained herein. While Research-publishing.net is committed to publishing works of integrity, the words are the authors' alone.

Trademark notice: product or corporate names may be trademarks or registered trademarks, and are used only for identification and explanation without intent to infringe.

Copyrighted material: every effort has been made by the editorial team to trace copyright holders and to obtain their permission for the use of copyrighted material in this book. In the event of errors or omissions, please notify the publisher of any corrections that will need to be incorporated in future editions of this book.

Typeset by Research-publishing.net
Cover illustration: © Tashatuvango - Adobe Stock.com
Cover design: © Raphaël Savina (raphael@savina.net)

ISBN13: 978-2-490057-31-3 (Ebook, PDF, colour)
ISBN13: 978-2-490057-32-0 (Ebook, EPUB, colour)
ISBN13: 978-2-490057-30-6 (Paperback - Print on demand, black and white)
Print on demand technology is a high-quality, innovative and ecological printing method; with which the book is never 'out of stock' or 'out of print'.

British Library Cataloguing-in-Publication Data.
A cataloguing record for this book is available from the British Library.

Legal deposit, UK: British Library.
Legal deposit, France: Bibliothèque Nationale de France - Dépôt légal: avril 2019.

Table of contents

v   Notes on contributors

1   Introduction
       Barbara Loranc-Paszylk

5   Occupying a new space: oral language skills within the disciplines in English-medium instruction
       Julia Hüttner

27   English as a lingua franca: an overview of communicative strategies
       Elwira Lewandowska

53   Acquisition of Japanese through translation
       Kinji Ito and Shannon M. Hilliker

75   Translation training and language instruction at the academic level
       Małgorzata Kodura

95   The infinitive in the writing of Czech advanced students of English
       Silvie Válková and Jana Kořínková

115   A search for paraphrasing and plagiarism avoidance strategies in the context of writing from sources in a foreign language
       Małgorzata Marzec-Stawiarska

137   Rethinking study abroad and intercultural competence
       Chesla Ann Lenkaitis

165   Author index

Notes on contributors

Editor

Barbara Loranc-Paszylk works as Assistant Professor at the University of Bielsko-Biała, Poland. She holds a PhD in applied linguistics from the University of Silesia. Her research interests focus on various aspects of telecollaboration as a way of pre-service teacher training, as well as innovative uses of digital resources in foreign languages teaching and learning. She has published in international journals and edited volumes in the field of second language acquisition.

Reviewers

Joanna Rokita-Jaśkow, PhD, is Associate Professor of applied linguistics at the Pedagogical University, Cracow, Poland. She specialises in child language acquisitions and language teacher education. She is an author of over 40 papers and 4 books in the field of SLA.

Linda Chmelařová, PhD, works at Palacký University in Olomouc. She primarily deals with organising English language courses for non-linguists in the faculty of education, i.e. students not majoring in teaching English as a foreign language. Her research focusses on improving future lower secondary teachers' language competencies and their language needs analysis. In her research, she is focussed on the role of translation in English language teaching (especially in the context of Czech-English structural differences) and students' translation skills. In her profession, she contributes to the development of international cooperation with the institute of foreign languages with universities mostly from western Europe. She also teaches language practise for primary students and participates in their evaluation.

Notes on contributors

Małgorzata Marzec-Stawiarska works as Assistant Professor at the Pedagogical University of Cracow, Poland. She holds a PhD in applied linguistics. Her research interests focus on developing writing and reading skills in a foreign language context, as well as the role of affective domain in learning languages. In her recent studies, she has investigated student strategies in academic and collaborative writing. She has also focussed on the issue of plagiarism in the academic writing of FL students.

Authors

Shannon M. Hilliker received her PhD at the University at Albany in curriculum and instruction with a focus on language learning in 2007. She has been in the TESOL (Teaching English to Speakers of Other Languages) field since 1999 where she has taught in both ESL (English as a Second Language) and teacher education. Dr Hilliker is Assistant Professor of TESOL at Binghamton University. Her research interests include rural education, teacher professional development, elementary ESL after school programmes, international student success, and online conversation and culture exchange.

Julia Hüttner is Professor in English Language Education at the University of Vienna, Austria, having moved there from the University of Southampton in 2018. Her main research interests lie in Content and Language Integrated Learning (CLIL), English Medium Instruction (EMI), and language teacher cognition. She also addresses the use of video resources to foster teacher learning and development. Her publications include a monograph, edited volumes, and numerous journal articles, and she is co-editor of *The Language Learning Journal*.

Kinji Ito is Lecturer in Japanese at the University of Pennsylvania. He received his MBA and PhD in Translation Studies from Binghamton University where he taught translation courses. Kinji also taught intensive language courses at the University of Massachusetts, Amherst, where he earned his MA in Japanese Language and Literature. His research interests lie primarily in the area of translation and language pedagogy.

Notes on contributors

Małgorzata Kodura is a certified translator in English and a translator trainer, employed as Assistant Professor at the Chair for Translator Education of the Institute of Modern Languages at the Pedagogical University of Cracow, where she teaches practical courses in translation and courses in translation theory. She holds a PhD in linguistics. Her scholarly interests in the area of translation studies focus on translator training and new technologies in translators' work.

Mgr. Jana Kořínková, PhD, teaches practical English language skills (pronunciation, speaking, and writing) and ELT methodology at the Institute of Foreign Languages, Palacký University in Olomouc, Czech Republic. Her research activities concentrate on analysing learners' written language as well as on effective teaching of advanced learners of English.

Chesla Ann Lenkaitis is Assistant Professor of Spanish at Binghamton University (Binghamton, New York, USA). She is the language coordinator of her department's introductory and intermediate language programme and also the programme coordinator of the Master of Arts in Teaching in French and Spanish Adolescence Education. Her research interests include identifying the most effective ways to learn and teach a second language (L2) and examining technology and intercultural competence in the L2 classroom.

Elwira Lewandowska works as Lecturer at the University of Bielsko-Biała. She is also a PhD candidate at Constantine the Philosopher University in Nitra, Slovakia. Her research interests include second language acquisition processes as well as teaching English as a Lingua Franca (ELF). She has published several works and now concentrates mainly on finishing her PhD project.

Małgorzata Marzec-Stawiarska works as Assistant Professor at the Pedagogical University of Cracow, Poland. She holds a PhD in applied linguistics. Her research interests focus on developing writing and reading skills in a foreign language context, as well as the role of affective domain in learning languages. In her recent studies, she has investigated student strategies in academic and collaborative writing. She has also focussed on the issue of plagiarism in the academic writing of FL students.

Notes on contributors

Silvie Válková is Associate Professor at the Faculty of Arts, Palacký University in Olomouc, Czech Republic. She has been teaching English grammar, academic English, and English for specific purposes for more than twenty years. Her fields of interest are interlanguage pragmatics and cross-cultural communication, focussing mainly on politeness strategies and their language manifestations.

Introduction

Barbara Loranc-Paszylk[1]

Learning foreign languages has always been an essential element of university education, although ways of providing linguistic instruction have been evolving to respond to the complex dynamics of social changes and expectations. For many decades in the modern age, language learning and teaching was conducted in the 'modernist' classroom (Kramsch, 2014) in which priority was given to standardised language tests and closely followed strict prescriptive norms of proper language use found in dictionaries and grammar books. This reality, the 'modernist' classroom, has been increasingly challenged by the new developments of the 21st century.

First, because of today's scale of migration and globalisation processes, the need to know more than one language has become even more pressing. Use of more than one language among individuals or communities "is as old as humanity, but multilingualism has been catapulted to a new world order in the 21st century" (Douglas Fir Group, 2016, p. 19). These new social and global developments have affected the language learning and teaching fields to an unprecedented extent.

Further to that, since the 1990's, research studies showed new socially oriented ways of effective language instruction addressed to the individual L2 learner (Benson, 2019). Following the critical assessment of cognitivism, the social turn in second language acquisition studies has been acknowledged (Block, 2003). Nevertheless, cognitivism which provides psychological explanations for L2 learning has still been used as an alternative approach to explore the processes of language learning and teaching (Ortega, 2011).

---

1. University of Bielsko-Biala, Bielsko-Biała, Poland; bloranc@ath.bielsko.pl

How to cite: Loranc-Paszylk, B. (2019). Introduction. In B. Loranc-Paszylk (Ed.), *Rethinking directions in language learning and teaching at university level* (pp. 1-4). Research-publishing.net. https://doi.org/10.14705/rpnet.2019.31.888

Introduction

Drawing on the abovementioned developments, this edited volume aims to offer valuable insights into how language learning and teaching processes have recently been supported, developed, and carried out within the university context. The chapters provide a timely focus on selected current issues related to learning and teaching languages at academic level, such as, for example: English medium programmes, communication processes in English as a lingua franca among participants of the Erasmus programmes, provision of English for professional and academic purposes, the role of corpora in cross-linguistic research to identify problematic language structures, or the impact of study abroad. As the studies presented in the book are embedded in several culturally diverse contexts, i.e. American, Austrian, Czech, and Polish, this volume may be of particular interest to international readers.

In the first chapter, **Julia Hüttner** focusses on the interface between language and content in bilingual education programmes involving English by investigating the notion of disciplinary language. While looking at data such as students' and teachers' perceptions of disciplinary language and students' oral production, she concludes that English medium instruction provides a unique framework that maximises development of student competences in the area of oral disciplinary language.

In the second chapter, **Elwira Lewandowska** recognises the importance of identifying communicative strategies used while communicating through English as a lingua franca. She presents the findings collected from interviews of international students participating in the Erasmus+ programme and claims that English as a lingua franca users may benefit from explicit teaching of communicative strategies.

In the third chapter, **Kinji Ito** and **Shannon M. Hilliker** focus on the role of translation as a vocabulary teaching technique in foreign language courses at university level. The authors discuss the results of a semester long study in which 21 learners of Japanese as a foreign language were learning Japanese vocabulary and conclude that intentional learning with the use of translation is significantly more effective in vocabulary learning and retention than incidental acquisition.

The fourth chapter by **Małgorzata Kodura** emphasises the role of explicit linguistic instruction in the translation training courses. In her study, the students who, while performing translation activities related to business texts, were given additional language related tasks, achieved better results and showed higher motivation.

The next two chapters deal with developing writing skills among university students. **Silvie Válková** and **Jana Kořínková**, while utilising the results of their cross-linguistic study, recognize the advantages of providing tailored instruction on a form of infinitive which does have a direct equivalent in students' L1 in order to improve their writing skills. **Małgorzata Marzec-Stawiarska** focusses on paraphrasing behaviours demonstrated by students when writing their MA dissertations in English. Having identified a group of before-writing, while-writing, and after-writing paraphrasing strategies, she concludes that explicit teaching of these strategies could be helpful for students in learning effective paraphrasing while writing from sources.

In the final chapter, **Chesla Ann Lenkaitis** recognises the value of short-term stay abroad on university students' development of intercultural communicative competence. She asserts that even a five day experience which includes numerous opportunities for authentic contact with L2 culture and L2 native speakers may result in a substantial development of intercultural communicative competence.

The chapters in this volume aim at allowing readers to get a better understanding of university students' linguistic needs and to explore a number of practical pedagogical implications for improvements in language learning and teaching within the university context.

References

Benson, P. (2019). Ways of seeing: the individual and the social in applied linguistics research methodologies. *Language Teaching, 52*(1), 60-70. https://doi.org/10.1017/S0261444817000234

Introduction

Block, D. (2003). *The social turn in second language acquisition*. Georgetown University Press.

Douglas Fir Group. (2016). A transdisciplinary framework for SLA in a multilingual world. *The Modern Language Journal*, *100*(S1), 19-47. https://doi.org/10.1111/modl.12301

Kramsch, C. (2014). Teaching foreign languages in an era of globalization: introduction. *The Modern Language Journal*, *98*(1), 296-311. https://doi.org/10.1111/j.1540-4781.2014.12057.x

Ortega, L. (2011). SLA after the social turn: where cognitivism and its alternatives stand. In D. Atkinson (Ed.), *Alternative approaches to second language acquisition* (pp. 179-192). Routledge.

1. Occupying a new space: oral language skills within the disciplines in English-medium instruction

Julia Hüttner[1]

Abstract

Bilingual education programmes involving English are currently experiencing an unprecedented rise in popularity, both at school and at university levels. While one of the aims of such educational programmes lies in developing both academic knowledge and language proficiency, our understanding of the interface between these two elements – language and content – is still developing. In this contribution I argue that one fruitful means of conceptualising this content and language interface is by focussing on disciplinary language, i.e. the language specific to a school subject or academic discipline. While the study of disciplinary literacies, with their prime consideration of reading and writing, has received some research attention (see e.g. Airey, 2011; Kuteeva & Airey, 2014), the more dynamic area of oral language in the subject classroom has been less focussed on. By drawing on an existing body of research, I show how disciplinary language within English Medium Instruction (EMI) is positioned by teachers and learners at both upper-secondary and tertiary levels of education. I place equal focus on two areas of research; firstly, I outline the perceptions of students and teachers towards (oral) disciplinary language, showing the difficulty of clearly positioning it on a continuum from 'language' to 'content' and the diverse interpretations of participants within EMI educational endeavours. The second area of research addresses student oral

---

1. University of Vienna, Vienna, Austria; julia.huettner@univie.ac.at

How to cite this chapter: Hüttner, J. (2019). Occupying a new space: oral language skills within the disciplines in English-medium instruction. In B. Loranc-Paszylk (Ed.), *Rethinking directions in language learning and teaching at university level* (pp. 5-26). Research-publishing.net. https://doi.org/10.14705/rpnet.2019.31.889

language production within the discipline. I show patterns of language production in terms of lexico-phraseological profiles of teacher talk and student production, as well as discourse-pragmatic analyses of patterns of argumentation and reasoning. The final section argues on the basis of these findings that EMI provides a unique potential of fostering student ability in the area of (oral) disciplinary language. Implications for practices in both secondary and tertiary EMI programmes focus on teacher education and classroom practices.

Keywords: English-medium instruction, tertiary education, upper-secondary education, subject-specific language, disciplinary language.

1. Introduction

The role of English as a truly global language is currently mirrored in the vibrancy of English Language Teaching (ELT) across the globe. In addition to generally rising numbers of English language learners and users, ELT is proliferating in terms of target learner groups which now in many contexts include professional and vocational, school-based education.

A special case in point in this diversification and expansion of ELT is the increased provision of English-medium programmes, both at school and university level, which add a complementary aspect to ELT. The proliferation of programmes using EMI[2] in non-Anglophone settings can be evidenced in the fact that now 26.9% of all EU universities offer such programmes – even if a caveat in the European context has to remain in that only a very small number of students are currently involved in such programmes, i.e. 1.3% (see Dearden, 2014; Wächter & Maiworm, 2014). Several North African countries

---

[2]. For the purposes of this paper, EMI is used as an umbrella-term to discuss all types of educational programmes that teach non-language subjects through English at primary, secondary, and tertiary levels of education. This terminological choice is not intended, however, to deny the important differences within EMI programmes; among the most noticeable of these are (1) the status of the student participants on a continuum of novices to experts of the academic content taught, (2) the linguistic homogeneity or heterogeneity of the student groups, and (3) the proficiency levels in English of both students and teachers.

are endorsing EMI as a means of fostering advanced English language skills and internationalising the young workforce (see, e.g. Havergal, 2016). In parallel with the establishment of English as official language of the Association of Southeast Asian Nations plus Japan, China and South Korea (ASEAN+3)[3], some ASEAN countries are now implementing top-down policies to foster EMI programmes at University level, for instance in Vietnam (Higher Education Reform Agenda, 2020). These developments at higher education institutions are bolstered by constantly rising student mobility; in the European context, this amounts to around a quarter of a million students annually on the EU-funded ERASMUS/SOCRATES programme, and the anglophone countries, as the most popular target destinations, attract a total of around 19% of its students from abroad (OECD, 2014; https://ec.europa.eu/programmes/erasmus-plus/about/statistics_en). These developments are mirrored at school level, where precise numbers of students taking part in English-taught programmes is harder to come by, but current overviews indicate that all EU countries offer some element of teaching through the medium of another language than the major educational one (in most cases, English) and the offer of EMI at schools is increasing also in public and private sectors in Asia and Latin America.

Despite this ongoing proliferation of EMI programmes at all levels, Wilkinson and Zegers's (2007) observation that these are "being introduced with scant underpinning of research findings" (p. 12) still holds true. What is especially characterised by a lack of specificity is the precise nature of EMI as a (language) educational endeavour and of the roles envisaged for or enacted through English within EMI. This is despite a growing research scene into EMI, which has also addressed language issues (e.g. Björkman, 2013; Doiz, Lasagabaster, & Sierra, 2013; Jenkins, 2014; Mauranen, 2012). With regard to educational studies into EMI programmes, I concur with Dafouz (2014) that these are "still mostly impressionistic" (p. 4). However, we do find outcome studies regarding general (foreign) language proficiency (e.g. Aguilar & Muñoz, 2013; Aguilar & Rodríguez, 2012) and, much less frequently, some studies investigated the effect of EMI on the learning outcomes in the respective academic subject content (see

---

3. See Article 34 of the Asean Charter (2008).

e.g. Dafouz, Camacho, & Urquia, 2014). Linked to this research activity, we can note that the key issue of the actual integration of 'language' and 'content' has only recently received more research attention (see, e.g. Llinares, 2015; Nikula, Dalton-Puffer, Llinares, & Lorenzo, 2016) and remains rather ill-defined in most EMI programmes. In practice, most programmes formulate only content aims explicitly and even the oft-cited 'dual focus' of Content and Language Integrated Learning (CLIL) (Coyle, Hood, & Marsh, 2010, p. 1) is mostly a programmatic criterion and not one enacted in practice.

Overall, we can note that these developments in ELT, most notably the rise of EMI programmes, have increased the link between learning English (as a foreign language) and professional practice (whether current or envisaged) or the academic study of non-language-related content. Thus, the 'traditional' motivators of foreign language learning, such as interest in (aspects) of the target culture(s), desire of travelling, broadening one's horizon, are being counterbalanced by an orientation towards disciplines and professions that use English, probably as a lingua franca, and which students of ELT wish to enter. In line with this, the target culture of language learning is no longer primarily the speech community or geographic entity, but rather the professional and/or disciplinary culture, which happens to use (also) English in their practices. This entails that the English taught and learnt is no longer only the language used for informal conversations, familiar matters or in literary outputs, but the language of the profession(s) or the discipline(s).

2. Disciplinary language as a site of language and content integration

By suggesting a focus on English as used for professional and academic purposes, it is necessary to acknowledge the vast body of research into English for Specific Purposes (ESP), including English for Academic Purposes (EAP). It is not the aim of this contribution to discuss the research and teaching traditions of ESP in any detail but it is worth noting that pinning down what is entailed by non-general language is by no means an easy task. Definitions of ESP generally focus on the needs of (adult) learners of English and imply a view of the specificity of "as language, skills, and genres appropriate to the [professional] activities the learners need to carry out in English" (Paltridge & Starfield, 2013, p. 2). The implication of much ESP research is that the language part of these activities can be separated out (at least in the teaching and learning phase) from socialisation into the professional or academic practices, and thus considers the content or disciplinary learning as a separate entity from the related language learning, as visualised in Figure 1 below.

Figure 1. Conceptualisation of language and content as separate (ESP)

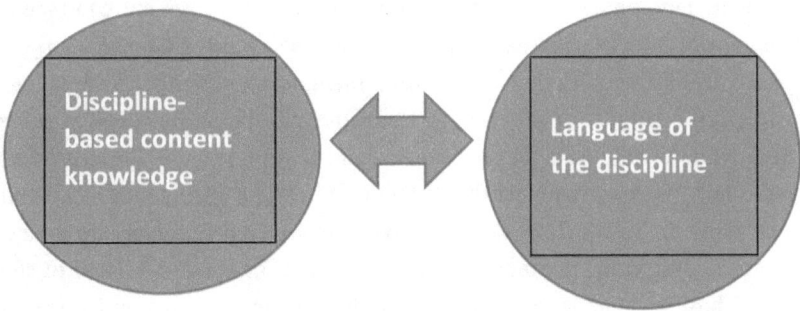

This conceptualisation helps capture the specificity of professional or academic language uses (see, e.g. Biber, 2006) and the relation of communicative purposes to textualisations within disciplines (see, e.g. Hyland, 2004; Swales, 2004). Some studies (e.g. Hüttner, 2007; Nesi & Gardner, 2012) have also conceptualised student text productions as independent learner genres. However, overall, the view of ESP entails a rather fixed conceptualisation of the specificity of English in the profession and does not fully represent the dynamic nature of concurrently learning new content and a foreign language, or indeed any language, for disciplinary purposes.

Indeed, the fact that language is the means of accessing school-based knowledge is well-established in a general educational context, leading to the view that "it is through language that school subjects are taught and through language that students' understanding of concepts is displayed and evaluated in school contexts" (Schleppegrell, 2004, p. 1). A host of work within L1-medium instruction has established the role of school in familiarising students with and socialising them into language uses that are more specific to their school-subjects (see for instance Mortimer & Scott, 2003).

I would argue that there is a fundamental integration of language and content learning, and that these two constructs cannot be viewed as separate monoliths, but are best considered as a fused entity, "a functioning or unified whole" (Collins & O'Brien, 2011, p. 241). Such a view challenges the independent status of, e.g. ESP, and proposes a much more disciplinary and integrated view of the learning of language and content. In this integration, several processes are combined in what is termed here 'disciplinary language use' (see Figure 2 below); firstly, the accessing of disciplinary knowledge through language, secondly, the learning of subject-specific language uses through the active reiteration practices of subject teachers while creating language/content learning affordances. These processes are essentially the same whether they take place in an L1-medium or L2-medium context. What does vary, however, is the extent to which participants are aware of these processes and the potential challenges related for learners related to some of them. Thus, both the learning and use of disciplinary language in L2-medium contexts constitutes a nexus of language and content integration in the participants' educational practices and hence an important focus for research activities.

Figure 2. Conceptualisation of language and content as integrated (disciplinary language)

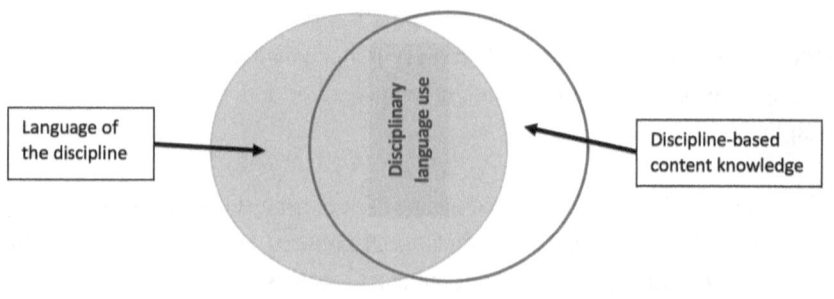

In the remainder of this contribution I present evidence from empirical studies into English-medium instruction programmes to highlight the ways in which English as a disciplinary[4] language constitutes such an integrated site of learning. Given the fact that written language in the disciplines has received research attention also in EMI contexts (see, e.g. Airey, 2011), I focus on the use of oral language in the disciplines.

3. Empirical studies: evidence for disciplinary language as a space fusing content and language

Nikula et al. (2016, pp. 7-9) suggest that there are three perspectives from which integration in CLIL, i.e. an L2-medium context, can be studied, namely classroom practices, participant views, and language management. In the present contribution, I focus on the first two of these aspects; to be more precise, I offer an overview and data samples of student production of disciplinary language, on the one hand, and of perception data of both students and teachers, on the other hand.

As mentioned above, I present research only into oral language use in the disciplines, which is characterised by generally allowing for less conscious planning and preparation, although there are also prepared presentations. Such a focus enables us to better capture developmental and learning processes surrounding disciplinary language, which seems particularly timely given the focus of much previous research on written texts.

The data presented here is drawn from five research projects in which I have been involved, which are referred to in this contribution by their acronyms, provided below.

---

4. Note that for ease of reading the terms disciplinary and subject-specific are used interchangeably in this contribution, although I acknowledge a distinction possible with the former referring to school subjects and the latter to university disciplines.

- AAIR[5]
- INTERLICA[6]
- CONCLIL[7]
- AME[8]
- HTL[9]

The first three of these, i.e. AAIR, INTERLICA, and CONCLIL, relate primarily to higher education contexts, and the final two, i.e. AME and HTL, to upper-secondary school education. The elements from these projects drawn upon below highlight the fusion of content and language use-and-learning in the use-and-learning of disciplinary language.

3.1. Evidence from perception data: teacher and learner beliefs on disciplinary language

The study of learner and teacher beliefs has become an established area of research within applied linguistics. Precise definitions and delimitations to related concepts, such as teacher cognition, folk linguistics, or subjective theories, are complex and, given the limitations of space, a discussion of these will not be provided here (but see Fives & Buehl, 2012 for an overview). For my purposes here, I adopt Barcelos's (2003, p. 8) summary definition of a cluster of beliefs surrounding language, language use, and language learning. Some general issues worth noting are that beliefs stand in a complex relationship to actions, and while there are well-documented levels of influence, it is simplistic

---

5. AAIR "Without English this is just not possible". Studies of language policy and practice in international universities from Europe and Asia, (2014-2015); funder: Annual Adventures in Research, University of Southampton (see Baker & Hüttner, 2017); sites: Austria, UK, Thailand.

6. INTERLICA "Internationalization of higher education in bilingual degrees: analysis of the linguistic, cultural and academic challenges" (2014-16) (http://www.ucm.es/interlica-en); funder: MINECO (The Spanish Ministry of Economics and Competitiveness) (see Dafouz, Hüttner, & Smit, 2018); site: Spain.

7. CONCLIL "Language and content integration: towards a conceptual framework" (2011-14) (PI Tarja Nikula); funder: Finnish Academy of Science (see Dafouz, Hüttner, & Smit, 2016); sites: Austria, Finland, Spain, UK.

8. AME "Learning to communicate in English in subject-specific ways: abilities and competences of Austrian CLIL students at upper secondary level" (2013-14); funder: Austrian Ministry of Education, Culture and the Arts HTL (see Hüttner & Smit, 2018); site: Austria.

9. HTL "Content and language integration at Austrian HTLS" (2007-2008); funder: Austrian Ministry of Education, Culture and Arts (PI Christiane Dalton-Puffer) (see Dalton-Puffer et al., 2008; Hüttner, Dalton-Puffer, & Smit, 2013); site: Austria.

to assume that holding a specific belief will result in actions aligned with it. The research reported on here adopts a view of beliefs as discursively (co-) constructed and in general focusses on professed beliefs (Speer, 2005), i.e. the beliefs teachers overtly state.

Data analysed within the AAIR project showed that across the university sites investigated in Austria, the UK, and Thailand, the lecturers believed that they were assessing *only content*, shown in comments such as

> "We don't evaluate English (.) these are no English essays".

> "When marking teachers won't focus on grammar they don't mind grammar mistakes as long as they understand what students mean" (Baker & Hüttner, 2017, p. 510).

The students at the same institutions, however, held much more diversified beliefs with an overall 46% (of a sample of 118 participants) opting for an affirmative when asked whether language was part of their assessments. There are differences between the individual sites with the one without any native speakers of English and with the highest level of self-assessed proficiency among the student group, i.e. Austria, least likely to consider English part of their EMI assessment. Interview data from the other two sites indicate that lecturers appear to classify elements of genre structure and discipline-related language conventions (including the need for academic language use) as part of 'content', whereas students seem to group these very same features within the cluster of 'language'.

Interviews with university teachers analysed in the AAIR (Baker & Hüttner, 2017) and ConCLIL (Dafouz, Hüttner, & Smit, 2016) projects suggest a cluster of beliefs shared across sites, although not among all participants. Most importantly, this is a view of English (as a disciplinary language) as something learnt implicitly through using the language as part of the community of practice at university. Thus, English as a disciplinary language is considered as something that needs to be learnt by both L1 and L2 students, and the added difficulty of being an L2 speaker is considered as variable depending on the discipline in question. Some disciplines, notably engineering, are considered as less language-intense with the connected belief that in those disciplines the disadvantage of being a non-native speaker of the medium of instruction is reduced.

Two projects presented here deal with secondary school contexts, both at upper levels and with professional orientation. In the technically oriented setting of the HTL data (Hüttner, Dalton-Puffer, & Smit, 2013), we find that the perception of a key difference of EMI (in this case CLIL) to regular English instruction at school is its relation to global English, to some extent conceptualised as English as a lingua franca, i.e. used with speakers of other languages than German or English and for purposeful communication. This use is by many participants equated with English for professional or disciplinary purposes. Thus, one person noted that CLIL is about "English as used for the job in technology" (Hüttner et al., 2013, p. 277). Further features of subject-specific language perceived by both the students and teachers in this context are the need for learning and using specific terminology. Frequently, mention is made of the role of glossaries, dictionaries, and vocabulary tests, but it does remain at times vague to what extent participants are referring to new *words* only or to both new words *and* new concepts that are being learnt and used. The teachers involved in the AME project, conducted also at an upper-secondary school within economics-related subjects, showed an awareness of some of the discipline-related discursive patterns, but overall perceived the learning of these to happen 'automatically' and so mirror the perceptions of tertiary level teachers (Hüttner & Smit, 2018). Thus, one AME teacher stated that

> "[The students] can manage that, that they transfer this [knowledge] communicatively (.) they're very skilled at that and they don't really need me for this transfer" (unpublished AME data).

In attempting to summarise the perception data from these projects on disciplinary language, we need to note firstly that a wide range of beliefs can be observed. Within all this diversity, however, some shared beliefs emerge:

- *Terminology is overtly perceived as a key feature of disciplinary language* (by both student and teacher participants). Learning terminology is generally seen as a conscious and direct endeavour. However, the delimitation of terminology and concepts is generally not clearly developed.

- *Discourse and genre features are not overtly perceived as part of disciplinary language.* The awareness of the existence of such discipline-specific features varies and is generally more pronounced at tertiary level. For many teachers, genre and discourse norms are tacitly seen as located within 'content' and are part of professional or disciplinary practices, i.e. indications of how things are done e.g. in engineering, in accounting, etc. Learning these is thus seen as a process of socialisation into disciplinary, professional, or relevant school practices. Some students share this perception, but for a group of student participants, discourse features were located within the (native) 'language' cluster of knowledge.

- *Perceptions of a link between disciplinary and native language remain inconclusive.* The university students in the UK and Thailand perceived adherence to native-speaker norms or, indeed, being a native speaker as inherently advantageous. Thus, they suppose that native speakers get better grades and that, generally, language proficiency is also assessed in their content-based assignments. At school level, within the Austrian CLIL context, a complementary view of locating native-speaker norms within general English as a foreign language classes and adherence to the norms of the discourse community within the CLIL or EMI classes prevails. Perceptions of the relationship between learning English based on native norms and on discourse-community norms are overall unclear.

3.2. Evidence from production data: classroom discourse

In this section, I bring together data focussing on the oral productions of students within EMI contexts. As far as possible, I thus aim to show some of the potential of EMI classrooms, that is to say, what is achievable by students in terms of disciplinary language. Secondly, I hope to provide some more evidence for disciplinary language as a nexus between language and content within these settings.

The first aspect of language production presented addresses terminology, and here I follow Nation (2016, p. 146) and define this as lexical items (including multi-word-units) characterising a subject or discipline in the sense of being used only, mainly, or with a specific meaning in this subject or discipline. The fact that terminology is very much in the awareness of both teachers and students as part of subject-specific or disciplinary language is borne out in the findings presented above. Linked to this is a frequent operationalisation of the knowledge of relevant terminology as a desired educational outcome. Moreover, a wealth of corpus linguistic studies highlights the specificity of the lexical profiles of individual disciplines (see, e.g. Chung & Nation, 2003). What is less clear, as mentioned earlier, is to what extent the learning and use of specific terminology in the foreign language constitutes an element of language learning (i.e. the new word) or of language-plus-concept learning (i.e. learning a new concept related to the subject *and* its correct term). Within the AME project, 70 different individual words and 52 multi-word units occurred in the spontaneous oral production of CLIL students[10]. A qualitative analysis of the classroom discourse shows that the student production of these items is at times clearly linked to learning the attached concepts.

As described above, the perceptions of genre or discourse structures as part of subject-specific language is much less clearly present in the awareness of key stakeholders in EMI. Nevertheless, specific patterns are observable also in oral production, but their use embodies both a desired outcome in terms of students producing texts in English that are seen as appropriate for the discipline and also part of the process of learning and being acculturated into the disciplinary discursive practices.

---

10. For a detailed discussion of the methodology of identifying subject-specific vocabulary, please see Rieder-Bünemann, Hüttner, and Smit (2018, forthcoming).

One such discourse pattern where the learning processes are foregrounded are the so-called language-related episodes (see Basturkmen & Shackleford, 2015), i.e. sections where language is topicalised within a generally subject teaching-oriented class. Most frequently, the focus of these episodes is terminological in nature, and so this provides a link to lexical learning. These stretches of classroom discourse encompass meaning-making in the form of clarifying specific terms and the accompanying concepts through provision of definitions, synonyms or translations. An example is the following extract, taken from the Interlica project (Dafouz, Hüttner, & Smit, 2018, p. 553):

> T: and behind the note (.) receivable or the note payable we will have a note
>
> S: and what is it?
>
> T: a note is a official document of payment (.) we say in Spanish letras de cambio okay? it's like a (.) it's like a (.) document, a official document in which you have a official stamp and it's like it's like money (…)

There have been some suggestions in the literature for over-arching frameworks within which the discourse patterns that are related specifically to academic disciplines are captured. One such framework underlying a number of research projects is *systemic functional linguistics* (see, for instance, Llinares & Whittaker, 2010; Llinares, Morton, & Whittaker, 2012) and more recently Dalton-Puffer (2013, 2016) has suggested *cognitive discourse functions* as a means of covering comprehensively the variety of functions, such as defining, explaining, etc., present in subject-specific discourse in CLIL. In the research presented here, the focus was on the interactive aspect of CLIL and EMI classroom discourse within oral classroom discourse and we focussed on argumentation in the AME project and on disciplinary reasoning in Interlica.

The school-based AME project addresses argumentation as a key practice in subject-specific discourse and we followed Nussbaum and Edwards's (2011) definition of it as a "process in which claims are made, supported, and evaluated by reasons and evidence" (p. 444). Claims, reasons, and evidence must adhere to subject-specific notions of acceptability; thus, for instance, anecdotal evidence is typically not deemed acceptable in the sciences. Also, the formulation of any argumentation needs to fulfil the criteria of appropriacy, often taught implicitly, active in the subject. In the context of social sciences that were studied in AME, the evaluation encompasses typically either a refutation of the claim itself (known as a counterclaim) or of the supporting evidence provided (known as a rebuttal). Using argumentation at school level aligns well with the aim of fostering critical thinking among students (Macagno, 2016) and more generally as a means towards an "enculturation into the scientific culture" (Jiménez-Aleixandre & Erduran, 2008, p. 4).

The analysis of the AME data led us to establish two distinct types of argumentation. Firstly, learning-focussed argumentation, which foregrounds the joint construction of subject knowledge and, secondly, expertise-focussed argumentation, which features a display of subject knowledge (see Hüttner & Smit, 2018). Thus, we can see that disciplinary language use in EMI contexts offers additional patterns to those observed in more expert disciplinary contexts; a learning-focussed argumentation is educational and shows an integrated moment of learning content and language through disciplinary language use. We can observe that in the learning-focussed argumentation, the teacher provides feedback on both the acceptability of the claims and evidence provided, often quite directly, but also provides recasts of the formulations suggested by students that correspond more clearly to conventions of language use in the subject. An example of a learning-focussed argumentation from AME is provided below (Hüttner & Smit, 2018, p. 294):

> T: so if you have a weaker currency of course uhm it is easier to export x exports become cheaper
>
> S: yeah for example great britain will buy something from Austria because we have a weaker currency but we won't buy something from great britain

T: uh i-if you say we won't buy <4>anything from great britain at all it's not true

S: yeah we we will buy but not not a lot

T: **uh not so uh we would probably be able to afford more if the currency was weaker you have to maybe put it that way right**

In the third turn, the teacher challenges the student to provide a more accurate account of the potential difference in trade occurring when the exporting country has a strong currency compared to the importer, which the student takes on in the fourth turn. The final turn (in bold here) shows the teacher recasting the accepted content of the student which, unusually, is also flagged explicitly as "you have to maybe put it that way[,] right".

At tertiary level, the project Interlica analysed the patterns of reasoning, i.e. providing disciplinary information in a logically linked format, in subject areas related to AME's, i.e. financial accounting and consumer behaviour. Details of the patterns observed are discussed in Dafouz et al. (2018), but what seems of most interest here is that within the learning process of the students, we can see how the content and language aspects are again merged. Thus, teachers scaffold students' understanding of the content issues through focussed questions and corrections, but also model – to some extent – the acceptable forms of presenting an argument, both orally, and of showing the ability to read specific genres, most notably in our data, the financial report. The following example, from Dafouz et al. (2018, pp. 556-557), highlights the scaffolding provided by the lecturer, given here in bold.

T: Pablo, **what do you think about this firm? (…) does it run well the business?**

[8 lines cut]

S: it makes more money with financing than with its xx operations

Chapter 1

> T: **it's bad (.) so you have to reorganize your firm. because if you are not doing money from your main activity, you have a problem**
>
> S: when operating activities is negative (.) is it always a bad situation?
>
> T: **it's a bad situation because you are not earning money (.) you are not doing money from your main activity(.) if you are a manufacture company, you are not doing well your business and you will have to reorganize the way to to run your business or (.) you have to change your business.** (.) okay? the the xx total is positive (.) but it's only your financial activity and your increases of capital (.) but it's only one period (.) but if you increase capital one period and what what will happen in the next period? we are losing money from our operating activities (.) right?

While the teacher, especially in the last turn presented here, uses terminology associated with financial accounting, the data show that the language-related appropriacy the lecturer appears to highlight is the correct production and interpretation of a financial report. We can argue, thus, that also here there is a bipartite classification possible of reasoning episodes focussed on enhancing student content understanding (as in the example above) and of expertise-focussed reasoning, in this case relegated to the written form.

In summary, the outsider's view shows that students produce disciplinary language in terms of terminology as well as discursive patterns in EMI contexts. The suggestion that disciplinary oral language acts as an interface of content and language learning, in addition to use, is especially apparent in the argumentation data; here we can see that there are two types of disciplinary language use; firstly, the expertise-focussed pattern, where a display of both disciplinary language and content knowledge is provided, and, secondly, the learning-focussed pattern, where accessing, learning, creating shared language, and content knowledge are foregrounded. Generally, we find that in the interactive classrooms we focussed on in this series of projects, the overarching learning and teaching frame appears to be one of socio-cultural learning, where the teacher provides support and scaffolding in guiding the students to a fuller disciplinary understanding.

4. Conclusions

This contribution argues that the traditional view of separating disciplinary content learning and use from the related (English) language learning and use, as is the case in an ESP conceptualisation, fails to capture the nexus where disciplinary language acts as a space where both content and language come together. Supporting evidence from both secondary and tertiary levels of English-medium instruction programmes has been provided. A linguistic analysis of student production data shows the interwoven nature of content and language in disciplinary discourse, and the way in which using a foreign language as medium of instruction brings this fusion to the foreground. Students access new disciplinary knowledge through language and also learn to present such knowledge in linguistically and content appropriate forms. Thus, a clear distinction between content and language becomes increasingly difficult, as discourse patterns, such as argumentation or reasoning depend on disciplinary norms, which enforce appropriacy both in terms of content and language. The perception data presented here highlight that this fusion is mirrored in difficulty of locating disciplinary language for the stakeholders. Thus, terminology tends to feature more on the 'language' side and discourse on the 'content' side, but teachers and students also have difficulty in deciding what is part of (English) language learning and what constitutes learning the broader conventions of the discipline. The data drawn together here also shows that there are still areas of contention, especially in the differences of perceptions of what is disciplinary language on the part of diverse participant groups, and that the distinction between 'general' language use and learning and disciplinary language use and learning still needs to be fine tuned.

The notion put forward here of disciplinary language as fusing content and language carries implications for teacher education. Firstly, there is a clear need to raise EMI teachers' awareness of the features of language use that constitute appropriacy in their discipline. Importantly, this will need to highlight the specific discourse patterns that exist, rather than only focussing on terminology. Secondly, teachers need to gain greater awareness of the dual nature of disciplinary discourse in the classroom, i.e. on the one hand, as a means of learning and, on the other hand, as a means of displaying knowledge. In this, it might be necessary to highlight that different levels of normativity apply, and that for the former, students might be encouraged to use their full linguistic repertoire to access new knowledge, whereas in the latter, students need to be told about the conventions that are at work in the various genres or texts produced in their disciplines.

References

Aguilar, M., & Muñoz, C. (2013). The effect of proficiency on CLIL benefits in engineering students in Spain. *International Journal of Applied Linguistics, 24*(1), 1-18. https://doi.org/10.1111/ijal.12006

Aguilar, M., & Rodríguez, R. (2012). Lecturer and student perceptions on CLIL at a Spanish university. *International Journal of Bilingual Education and Bilingualism, 15*(2), 183-197. https://doi.org/10.1080/13670050.2011.615906

Airey, J. (2011). The disciplinary literacy discussion matrix: a heuristic tool for initiating collaboration in higher education. *Across the disciplines, 8*(3). https://wac.colostate.edu/docs/atd/clil/airey.pdf

Asean Charter. (2008). The working language of ASEAN shall be English. http://asean.org/storage/images/archive/publications/ASEAN-Charter.pdf

Baker, W., & Hüttner, J. (2017). English and more: a multisite study of roles and conceptualisations of language in English medium multilingual universities from Europe to Asia. *Journal of Multilingual and Multicultural Development, 38*(6), 501-516. https://doi.org/10.1080/01434632.2016.1207183

Barcelos, A. M. F. (2003). Researching beliefs about SLA: a critical review. In P. Kalaja & A.M.F. Barcelos (Eds), *Beliefs about SLA: new research approaches* (pp. 7-33). Springer. https://doi.org/10.1007/978-1-4020-4751-0_1

Basturkmen, H., & Shackleford, N. (2015). How content lecturers help students with language: an observational study of language-related episodes in interaction in first year accounting classrooms. *English for Specific Purposes, 37*, 87-97. https://doi.org/10.1016/j.esp.2014.08.001

Biber, D. (2006). *University language: a corpus-based study of spoken and written registers* (vol. 23). John Benjamins Publishing. https://doi.org/10.1075/scl.23

Björkman, B. (2013). *English as an academic lingua franca*. De Gruyter Mouton.

Chung, T. M., & Nation, P. (2003). Technical vocabulary in specialised texts. *Reading in a foreign language, 15*(2), 103-116.

Collins, J. W., & O'Brien, N. P. (2011). *The Greenwood dictionary of education*. ABC-CLIO.

Coyle, D., Hood, P., & Marsh, D. (2010). *Content and language integrated learning*. Ernst Klett Sprachen.

Dafouz, E. (2014). Integrating content and language in European higher education: an overview of recurrent research concerns and pending issues. In A. Psaltou-Joycey, E. Agathopoulou & M. Mattheoudakis (Eds), *Cross-curricular approaches to language education* (pp. 289-304). Cambridge Scholars.

Dafouz, E., Camacho, M., & Urquia, E. (2014). 'Surely they can't do as well': a comparison of business students' academic performance in English-medium and Spanish-as-first-language-medium programmes. *Language and Education, 28*(3), 223-236. https://doi.org/10.1080/09500782.2013.808661

Dafouz, E., Hüttner, J., & Smit, U. (2016). University teachers' beliefs of language and content integration in English-medium education in multilingual university settings. In T. Nikula, E. Dafouz, P. Moore & U. Smit (Eds), *Conceptualising integration in CLIL and multilingual education* (pp. 123-143). Multilingual Matters. https://doi.org/10.21832/9781783096145-009

Dafouz, E., Hüttner, J., & Smit, U. (2018). New contexts, new challenges for TESOL: understanding disciplinary reasoning in oral interactions in English-medium instruction (EMI). *TESOL Quarterly, 52*(3), 540-563. https://doi.org/10.1002/tesq.459

Dalton-Puffer, C. (2013). A Construct of cognitive discourse functions for conceptualising content-language integration in CLIL and multilingual education. *European Journal of Applied Linguistics 1*(2), 216-253. https://doi.org/10.1515/eujal-2013-0011

Dalton-Puffer, C. (2016). Cognitive discourse functions: specifying an integrative interdisciplinary construct. In T. Nikula, E. Dafouz, P. Moore & U. Smit (Eds), *Conceptualising integration in CLIL and multilingual education* (pp. 29-54). Multilingual Matters.

Dalton-Puffer, C., Hüttner, J., Jexenflicker, S., Schindelegger, V., & Smit, U. (2008). Content and language integrated learning an Österreichs Höheren Technischen Lehranstalten. Vienna: Bundesministerium für Unterricht, Kultur und Kunst, Abt. II/2 [Austrian Ministry of Education, Culture and Art, Section II/2].

Dearden, J. (2014). *English as a medium of instruction – a growing global phenomenon*. British Council. https://www.britishcouncil.org/education/ihe/knowledge-centre/english-language-higher-education/report-english-medium-instruction

Doiz, A., Lasagabaster, D., & Sierra, J. M. (2013). *English-medium instruction at universities: global challenges*. Multilingual Matters.

Fives, H., & Buehl, M. M. (2012). Spring cleaning for the "messy" construct of teachers' beliefs: What are they? Which have been examined? What can they tell us. *APA educational psychology handbook, 2*, 471-499. https://doi.org/10.1037/13274-019

Havergal, C. (2016, September 24th). Maghreb turns to English to tackle graduate unemployment. *Times Higher Education*.

Hüttner, J. (2007). *Analysing student texts*. Peter Lang.

Hüttner, J., Dalton-Puffer, C., & Smit, U. (2013). The power of beliefs: Lay theories and their influence on the implementation of CLIL programmes. *International Journal of Bilingual Education and Bilingualism, 16*(3), 267-284. https://doi.org/10.1080/13670050.2013.777385

Hüttner, J., & Smit, U. (2018). Negotiating political positions: subject-specific oral language use in CLIL classrooms. *International Journal of Bilingual Education and Bilingualism, 21*(3), 287-302. https://doi.org/10.1080/13670050.2017.1386616

Hyland, K. (2004). *Disciplinary discourses: social interactions in academic writing*. University of Michigan Press.

Jenkins, J. (2014). *English as a lingua franca in the international university. The politics of academic English language policy*. Routledge.

Jiménez-Aleixandre, M. P., & Erduran, S. (2008). Argumentation in science education: an overview. In S. Erduran & M. P. Jiménez-Aleixandre (Eds), *Argumentation in science education: perspectives from classroom-based research* (pp. 3-27). Springer.

Kuteeva, M., & Airey, J. (2014). Disciplinary differences in the use of English in higher education: reflections on recent language policy developments. *Journal of Higher Education, 67*(5), 533-549. https://doi.org/10.1007/s10734-013-9660-6

Llinares, A. (2015). Integration in CLIL: a proposal to inform research and successful pedagogy. *Language, Culture and Curriculum, 28*(1), 58-73. https://doi.org/10.1080/07908318.2014.1000925

Llinares, A., Morton, T., & Whittaker, R. (2012). *The roles of language in CLIL*. Cambridge University Press.

Llinares, A., & Whittaker, R. (2010). Writing and speaking in the history class: a comparative analysis of CLIL and first. *Language use and language learning in CLIL classrooms, 7*, 125.

Macagno, F. (2016). Argument relevance and structure. Assessing and developing students' uses of evidence. *International Journal of Educational Research, 79*, 180-194. https://doi.org/10.1016/j.ijer.2016.07.002

Mauranen, A. (2012). *Exploring ELF: academic English shaped by non-native speakers*. Cambridge University Press.

Mortimer, E. F., & Scott, P. H. (2003). *Meaning making in secondary science classrooms*. Open University Press.

Nation, I. S. P. (2016). *Making and using word lists for language learning and testing*. John Benjamins. https://doi.org/10.1075/z.208

Nesi, H., & Gardner, S. (2012). *Genres across the disciplines: student writing in higher education*. Cambridge University Press.

Nikula, T., Dalton-Puffer, C., Llinares, A., & Lorenzo, F. (2016). More than content and language: the complexity of integration in CLIL and multilingual education. In T. Nikula, E. Dafouz, P. Moore & U. Smit (Eds), *Conceptualising integration in CLIL and multilingual education* (pp. 1-25). Multilingual Matters. https://doi.org/10.21832/9781783096145-004

Nussbaum, E. M., & Edwards, O. V. (2011). Critical questions and argument stratagems: a framework for enhancing and analyzing students' reasoning practices. *Journal of the Learning Sciences, 20*, 443-488. https://doi.org/10.1080/10508406.2011.564567

OECD. (2014). Indicator C4: who studies abroad and where? In *Education at a glance 2014: OECD Indicators*. OECD Publishing. https://doi.org/10.1787/888933118656

Paltridge, B., & Starfield, S. (Eds). (2013). The handbook of English for specific purposes. Wiley-Blackwell.

Rieder-Bünemann, A., Hüttner, J., & Smit, U. (2018). The potential of CLIL: students' use of subject-specific terminology. *CELT Matters* 2. https://celt.univie.ac.at/home/celt-matters-online-journal/current-volume/

Rieder-Bünemann, A., Hüttner, J., & Smit, U. (forthcoming). Capturing technical terms in spoken CLIL: a holistic model for identifying subject-specific vocabulary.

Schleppegrell, M. J. (2004). *The language of schooling: a functional linguistic perspective*. Lawrence Erlbaum Associates.

Speer, N. M. (2005). Issues of methods and theory in the study of mathematics teachers' professed and attributed beliefs. *Educational studies in Mathematics, 58*(3), 361-391. https://doi.org/10.1007/s10649-005-2745-0

Swales, J. (2004). *Research genres: explorations and applications*. Cambridge University Press. https://doi.org/10.1017/CBO9781139524827

Wächter, B., & Maiworm, F. (2014). *English-taught programmes in European higher education: the State of play in 2014*. Lemmens.

Wilkinson, R., & Zegers, V. (2007). *Researching content and language integration in higher education*. Valkhof Pers.

2 English as a lingua franca: an overview of communicative strategies

Elwira Lewandowska[1]

Abstract

The present contribution discusses the importance of communicative strategies in introducing English as a Lingua Franca (ELF). A brief meta-analysis of the research conducted in the area of pragmatics reveals that one of the most salient elements of using ELF is the users' ability to conduct meaningful exchanges through various communicative strategies. The results of the case study show that certain strategies are less favoured by ELF users, like those that seem to require manipulation of the language content and adjusting the language forms to meet the goals of communication. It is also demonstrated that contrary to the results of the meta-analysis, the participants of the study use all types of strategies: avoidance, compensation, and stalling without easily observable differences in the gathered results. The analysis of the results allows us to claim that incorporating communicative strategies should be of importance in considering the possibility of teaching ELF or at least allowing the learners of the English language to explore various strategies that may be proved as useful in their language use in a global marketplace.

Keywords: English as a lingua franca, English as a foreign language, communicative strategies, effective communication.

---

1. University of Bielsko-Biala, Bielsko-Biała, Poland; elewandowska@ath.bielsko.pl

How to cite this chapter: Lewandowska, E. (2019). English as a lingua franca: an overview of communicative strategies. In B. Loranc-Paszylk (Ed.), *Rethinking directions in language learning and teaching at university level* (pp. 27-52). Research-publishing.net. https://doi.org/10.14705/rpnet.2019.31.890

Chapter 2

1. Introduction

The new linguistic reality involves finding ways of communication in the globalised environment, where people move all around the world in order to find work, learn, or share experiences. Consequently, just as Hülmbauer, Böhringer, and Seidlhofer (2008) put it, we need to: "find a common voice in order to bridge language barriers" (p. 26). Therefore, it seems salient to find the ways that would help in bridging communication between people of different mother tongues and different cultures.

The choice of a language that becomes a *lingua franca*, so merely the language of communication between people who do not share a common native language of communication (Richards, Platt, & Weber, 1985), is always linked with many socio-cultural, and probably, more importantly, political reasons. The promotion of English worldwide that resulted in English becoming the new *lingua franca* has many economic, cultural, and social causes, but it is a fact that: "English has been successfully promoted, and has been eagerly adopted in the global linguistic marketplace" (Phillipson, 1992, p. 7).

ELF transcends the boundaries and allows for constant variation that is the result of the user's backgrounds, both linguistic and sociocultural, which influence their performance. Although in the works of Jenkins (2000), Seidlhofer (2005), Breiteneder (2005), or Dewey (2006), certain repetitive regularities of ELF have been discovered, they did not result in ELF becoming a codified variety and is still far from being treated as a norm. However, it seems that there are certain suggestions concerning introducing certain aspects of ELF into the teaching programmes (Lopriore & Vettorel, 2016; Llurda, Bayyurt, & Sifakis, 2018). These would include raising teachers' awareness about English and those ELF elements that are already recognised as prevailing in the *lingua franca* context.

In this sense, communicative strategies that are employed by ELF users should be given more attention by teachers. Drawing on the research findings concerned with regards to the most common strategies that are characteristic in ELF communication can be considered practical and helpful for English language learners. When teachers of English know which strategies prevail, they can allow their students to deal with the changing environment of English use worldwide with accordance to the very needs of students concerning communication in the *lingua franca* context. Therefore, before a meta-analysis of ELF communicative strategies is presented, salient information concerning the theory of Language Learning Strategies (LLS) and their importance in foreign language teaching and learning will be presented.

2. Literature review

2.1. Language learning strategies

LLS have been defined by Scarcella and Oxford (1992) as "specific actions, behaviors, steps, or techniques such as seeking out conversation partners, or giving oneself encouragement to tackle a difficult language task used by students to enhance their own learning" (p. 63). Consequently, employing such techniques by the learners allows them to deal with language learning more effectively. The notion of LLS hence deals with the possible individual approaches employed by the learners during the process of second language learning that can have positive outcomes in their performances.

The notion of LLS, however, seems to be less examined nowadays, which can be linked with the fuzziness of the definitions related to this concept and certain discrepancies concerning conceptualisation of the notion (Gu, 2012). There are almost 24 different descriptions of LLS (Horváthová, 2013), and it seems that the attempts to put the strategies in fitting categories were rather fruitless. Macaro (2006) claims that the researchers cannot agree on matters such as the classification of strategies into clear groups or frameworks, and Gu (2012) claims that some concepts share the name, however, differ in meaning, and scholars are presenting opposite views when even describing the notion of a language strategy itself. Yet, regardless of the definitional conundrum, we may briefly conclude that LLS refer to the situation when learners undertake various steps (either externally observable or referring to mental processes) to achieve measurable language benefits (in terms of skills). As it was explained, learning strategies can be divided into several types that will vary on the basis of which taxonomy is employed by the researcher. Therefore, in this paper, only communicative strategies will be presented in detail. Such a choice results from the fact that ELF is a communicative phenomenon, thus users of ELF must know and employ various communicative strategies that provide them with a chance of having a successful communicative exchange. It seems obvious then if one wants to increase the chances of effective communication, he or she should be able to effectively use the strategies that are of help and prevail among ELF users.

2.2. Communicative strategies

According to Dörnyei (1995), L2 communication poses a lot of possible problems for the interlocutors. To tackle them, one may employ a range of verbal and non-verbal strategies that may foster communication. Although, as it was mentioned above, there is a lack of complete consensus on how to define communicative strategies, a working definition proposed by Corder (1981), in which communicative strategies are defined as techniques that are of help when a communication breakdown is to be avoided, seems to cover our understanding of the phenomenon in question. According to Dörnyei (1995, p. 58), comprising Váradi (1980), Tarone (1977), Færch and Kasper (1983), and Białystok's (1990) principles, by following a traditional conceptualisation of the term, communicative strategies can be divided into three main types of strategies: avoidance or reduction, achievement or compensation, and stalling or time gaining tactics. The avoidance or reduction strategies comprise two sub-strategies: strategy of not putting the message forward due to insufficient language skills, or leaving the message without a logical continuation or end. Achievement or compensation strategies comprise such actions as:

- circumlocution, by the use of which the interlocutor provides a definition rather than the concrete word that is needed;

- approximation which refers to the use of those vocabulary items that are close in meaning to the target words;

- the use of words that denote a general category of words, when context specific words are lacking;

- creating new words on the basis of some presumed rules;

- the use of body language;

- calques from L1;

- attempts to use vocabulary items in a manner to make them sound as words of foreign origin; and

- switching between two linguistic codes and finally asking for some help in finishing the message.

The last type of communicative strategies – stalling and time gaining tactics – comprises the use of filled pauses or lexical fillers in order to have time to think about the utterance.

Regardless of the fact that the presented division is broad, it serves the purpose of this paper and namely allows us to investigate the use of communicative strategies among ELF users on the basis of the existent research in a form of a meta-analysis and furthermore, allows us, although somewhat briefly, to investigate the use of communicative strategies among ELF users in our own case study.

Research concerning the use of communicative strategies among L2 users indicates that they are effective in increasing the chances of involving themselves in a meaningful communicative exchange, especially when they lack the linguistic means to put the message forward. The study of Dobao and Martínez (2007) revealed that both native and non-native users of L2 try to use some strategies that may enhance communication. Moreover, there is a correlation between the level of proficiency in a given language and the dependence on the use of strategies. In other words, the lower the level is, the higher the use of strategies seems to be (Dobao & Martínez, 2007; Terrel, 1977).

There are also studies aimed at identifying the use of communicative strategies among international learners of English as a foreign language. The study conducted by Tan, Fariza, and Jaradat (2012) revealed that code-switching is the most commonly used strategy by the international learners of English according to their self-reported claims, whereas word coinage was the least common one. Moreover, the study conducted by Nakatani (2005) reveals that strategy training may improve the overall spoken competence of L2 users. Such training helps the learners to use more of achievement or compensation strategies, and less of the avoidance ones. In a similar study of Rabab'ah (2015) in which the author investigated the usefulness of strategy training on learners' performances, it was revealed that "participants in the strategy training group significantly outperformed the control group in their IELTS speaking test scores" (p. 625). We can conclude that communicative strategies are crucial in developing learners' skills and that training may significantly improve their overall spoken competence. In the attempts aimed at introducing ELF into teaching policies, the importance of incorporating communicative strategies seems to be of even greater importance.

2.3. Communicative strategies employed by ELF users

What transpires through ELF research is that although no propositions concerning teaching it are put forward by the researchers in a straightforward manner, some suggestions derived from the nature of ELF in face of the research done so far call for some changes in English Language Teaching (ELT) concerning pedagogical implications of ELF nowadays. In terms of international communication, the users of English are faced with an "unpredictable variability" (Maley, 2009, p. 191); the situations in which the sociolinguistic elements of L1 impact communication in L2. Our students must be prepared for it in order to enhance their chances for effective and sufficient communication. ELF encompasses the sociolinguistic changes, as its main feature is to promote communication in an international setting among speakers of different L1, which does not necessarily mean acquiring a native-like proficiency (Seidlhofer, 2001).

The strategies people use in general while involved in ELF communicative exchanges may extend mainly to the use of communicative strategies. Such knowledge, as a consequence, may be of help for learners of English that will be forced to deal with the 'fluid' nature of ELF that is, whether we like it or not, a linguistic reality.

Although in general, when it comes to learning foreign languages, the use of various direct and indirect strategies may enhance the ultimate outcome of language education, from an ELF perspective in which ELF is used but yet not taught, communication strategies seem to be even more important for their users. A meta-analysis of the existent research on ELF pragmatics with the main aim of pointing to the use of communicative strategies of ELF users will be of importance in the following sub-section.

2.4. Avoidance strategies used by ELF users

What can be observed in the research on the use of English in the *lingua franca* context is that ELF users go to any lengths to put the message forward. Research conducted by Pitzl (2005) revealed that ELF users tend to present a high level of cooperation aimed at sustaining meaningful communication. Through the negotiation of meaning, they approach communication creatively and because of that are able to deal with problems that are present in communicative exchanges more easily. Moreover, Mauranen (2006), while investigating the characteristic features of communicative exchanges between ELF users, found out that through 'pro-active' work that entails various strategic practices used by the speakers, they are able to communicate more effectively. It seems that in terms of communication in ELF, the avoidance strategies are not of much help and as such introducing them to learners, as well as adapting them, is not desired. Communication in ELF is aimed at putting the message forward and achieving mutual goals. In a situation when both parties use a language that is not their L1, it seems that avoidance techniques would not result in mutual intelligibility, but rather cause communication breakdowns. That is why ELF users tend to employ compensation strategies more often.

2.5. Compensation strategies used by ELF users

Studies conducted by Lichtkoppler (2007), Watterson (2008), and Cogo (2009) revealed that a common strategy employed by ELF users is repetition and paraphrasing. Both practices seem to be common ways aimed at dealing with communication breakdowns (Cogo & Dewey, 2006), especially if prolonged silence occurs. Therefore, what should be made clear for ELF users is that circumlocution strategies may be helpful. Presenting the importance of such a strategy seems to be a fair choice in raising awareness of ELF among international users.

Another strategy that must be recognised and should be used by ELF speakers is code-switching, which along with coining new words and foreignising mother-tongue words, seems to be commonly used and is corroborated in research. Hülmbauer (2013) in her investigation showed that ELF speakers make an active use of their L1 nativeness. It means that L1 is far more important in ELF communication than it is in using English as a foreign language. The techniques that are common are code-switching, transferring of L1 words to L2, and changing them in a fashion aimed at making them 'sound' foreign. What can be also observed is an increased use of cognates. A fact worth mentioning is that code-switching serves a more important purpose than just to sustain mutual intelligibility, as it also signals speakers' cultural values (Klimpfinger, 2007). What can be drawn from this, is that ELF users must be aware of the fact that making use of their bilingual or even plurilingual resources is something desired in the *lingua franca* context, contrary of employing such techniques in using English as a foreign language, which is considered a mistake. Yet again, creating a positive image of L1 that influences and can be of help in using ELF seems to be a desired practice in the *lingua franca* context.

One of the communicative strategies introduced by Dörnyei (1995) is time-gaining tactics. In terms of ELF communication, it seems important to mention the usefulness and commonness of such a strategy. Böhringer (2007), while investigating the role of silent and filled pauses in ELF, revealed that apart from the fact that they are common resources, ELF users turn to when they face communicative obstacles in order to find how to effectively put the message forward. They also have an important role in creating meaning in ELF exchanges.

As it was presented above, the studies concerning communicative strategies in the *lingua franca* context are mainly focussed on ELF users. Choi and Jeon's (2016) claim that "ELF pedagogy has been mostly discussed at only a conceptual level and pedagogical research is scarce" (p. 1) seems to be in line with such an assumption. That is why the study conducted by Dimoski, Yujobo, and Imai (2016) in the context of the Association of Southeast Asian Nations, which focussed on the effectiveness of communicative strategies training in the pro-active listening activities in ELF-based pedagogical contexts, seems both extremely interesting and important. In the study, 53 students, who actively participated in an English class at the *Center for English as a Lingua Franca* at Tamagawa University, were trained to use communicative strategies in pro-active listening comprehension activities. According to their self-reported claims, their ability to tackle miscommunication was increased by over 20 percent due to training. The authors of the study claim that: "ELF pedagogy should incorporate opportunities for students to explicitly learn and use [communicative strategies] independently to become competent international communicators among other ELF speakers" (Dimoski et al., 2016, p. 67). It is up to our understanding that the effective use of communicative strategies, can indeed increase the ability to sustain meaningful communication among all international users of English worldwide.

What can be concluded at this point is that ELF users employ communicative strategies very often when they are involved in spoken exchanges with other non-native speakers of English. Therefore, raising awareness of such strategies, as well as allowing the learners to practice them on their own studying seems to be of a high importance. The nature of ELF, which makes it an emergent phenomenon that is influenced by its users to a high degree (by their L1, culture, social background, personal language preferences, style, etc.), makes it hardly teachable at this point. Regardless, allowing students to become accustomed to all the intricate details of ELF use concerning its lexicogrammar, phonology and pragmatics should be desired by the educators and learners themselves,

Chapter 2

as for now, it is a fair assumption to be made that ELF findings are of great importance for ELT. And because ELF research may not result in ELF being defined as a variety, and as such will not be introduced in the curricula, it must not be a limitation for the teachers and learners. At this point, a pivotal point of ELF research should be raising awareness of its importance in worldwide communication.

2.6. The importance of communicative strategies in teaching English in the new era of global communication

The changes in the way scholars approach language can be explained not only on the basis of the inevitable changes of students' needs in relation to their language knowledge but also in the nature of knowledge concerning the study of languages itself (Richards & Rodgers, 2001). In other words, the more is known about the language itself, the more it results in a shift in the way a language must be taught. Moreover, students' needs are also salient elements of language changes, as the nature of language use has been transformed from a rather passive knowledge to an active use of language in the international environment. That is why, knowledge concerning language use is in a state of flux, with new ideas being created worldwide that aim at improving the ways in which language is acquired (Turula, 2010). Yet, language education was and still is associated with a significant attachment to the traditional conception of language as a property of its native speakers. The creators of traditional, humanistic, and communicative methods were more interested in providing ideas and explanations of their utility, rather than being interested in assessing the increasing role of English as an international language. Although the incorporation of ELF and its main paradigms into methods of language teaching and learning should resemble the changes of the evolving nature of English and the needs of the students in the global marketplace, the reality seems to contradict such an assumption. In the ELF context,

> "mastery of the system (or perhaps better systems), needs to involve developing the ability to use the linguistic resources of English in an especially flexible way. The notion of inclusion in a lingua franca

community should relate not to conformity to a predetermined set of [English as a new language] norms, but to a speaker's ability to converge towards an interlocutor as the communication progresses moment by moment" (Dewey, 2006, p. 230).

This requires not only creativity and openness, so cherished in the scope of humanistic, communicative, and post-methods and approaches, but firstly knowledge of the evolving nature of English in the 21st century. Maybe, the increased reluctance to acknowledge the fact that English is no longer a singular property of it native speakers does not come only from the fact that language is usually seen a cultural product of a given community, but as Dewey (2006) suggests, following Pavlenko's (2002) statements, that the strong objections towards rejection of standardised forms come from "a broad postmodern tradition of questioning current paradigms" (cf Pavlenko's (2002) discussion of poststructuralist approaches to social factors in second language acquisition, in Dewey, 2006, p. 192). The position of English worldwide has changed, and we should try to accommodate to these changes. If we want to prepare our students for a bright future, they must be able to communicate effectively in the *lingua franca* context, where communicative conventions differ from those established by the native users of English. And definitely, by pointing to the importance of communicative strategies, and focussing on those that prevail in the lingua franca context, we may help our students in becoming successful users of English.

The presented meta-analysis of ELF research allowed us to identify various strategies employed by ELF users in *lingua franca* communication. By analysing the available and approachable research papers it was possible to conclude that the strategies used by ELF users fall into the category of communicative ones.

3. The study

In order to provide insights into the presented issues, a case study was designed to investigate the use of communicative strategies by the users of ELF (in this case non-native users of English in a foreign language environment for whom English is the only language of communication). It seems salient to investigate the use of communicative strategies by the ELF users in order to establish which strategies are the most common when communicating in the *lingua franca* context and if there an observable tendency among the ELF users towards a particular type of the communicative strategies. Therefore, an exploratory research question was created: which strategies are employed by ELF users and what is the frequency of use of communicative strategies among them?

It is hypothesised by the author that ELF users must deal with a high level of unpredictability in terms of oral communication due to ELF's fluid end emergent nature. That is why the participants should present a strong inclination towards the use of various strategies, ranging from the ones requiring some form of language manipulation such as approximation, circumlocution, or creating new words, and the ones that are more related to a person's attitude such as time gaining tactics, gestures, or asking for help. It is also hypothesised that the participants may show certain preferences towards the use of compensation strategies in place of the ones that require avoidance, as it is suggested by the existing research concerning the pragmatic competences of ELF users.

3.1. Methodology

The study adopts a qualitative data collection technique – an asynchronous structured online interview. Drawing on Dörnyei's (1995) framework comprising Váradi (1980), Tarone (1977), Færch and Kasper (1983), and Białystok's (1990) principles, this study aims to investigate the use of communicative strategies among the ELF users. The participants were presented with various communicative scenarios, all of them arranged in such a way to present a given communicative strategy and asked whether they employ them while involved in a communicative exchange. They were also asked about the frequency of use of a given strategy if it was indicated as used and four questions concerning their general attitude towards communication in English, especially language problems, were elicited. The participants were also asked to answer questions concerning their personal background such as their age, language level, knowledge of other languages, and years of language education. The interview was devised in English, as all participants conduct their studies in English as it is for them the language of instruction.

3.2. Participants

The study was based on the data collected from six participants – all of whom are university students – three women and three men. The average age of the participants was 22; the average time spent on school education and language education was 13 years. The majority of the respondents reported that they are on the B2 level (66%); one stated that she knows English at C1 level (16 %) and one on B2/C1 level (16%) when it comes to their self-perceived language proficiency.

The participants were the Erasmus students studying in Poland coming from different countries (Spain, Bulgaria, and Turkey), conducting their studies in the interdisciplinary model for whom English was the language of instruction.

- **P1** – the first participant was a 23-year-old student from Spain. She has been learning English since she was seven years old. Her self-perceived level of English is B2. She knows Bulgarian on a C2 level, and Polish on an A1 level. She agrees that English is a modern *lingua franca*, and claims that she mainly communicates in English with native speakers.

- **P2** – the second participant was a 21-year-old student from Spain. He has been learning English since the first grade of primary school. His self-perceived level of English is B2/C1. He knows French at an A2/B1 level and is fluent in Galician. He agrees that English is a modern *lingua franca*, and claims to use it with non-native speakers more.

- **P3** – the third participant was a 21-year-old student from Spain. She has been learning English for 15 years. Her self-perceived level of English is C1. She knows Basque at a C1 level and French at a B2 level. She agrees that English is a modern *lingua franca* and claims to use it with non-native speakers more.

- **P4** – the fourth participant was a 21-year- old student from Turkey who has been studying English for six years only. His self-perceived level of English is B2. He knows Spanish but he has not specified the level. He disagrees that English is a modern *lingua franca*, yet claims that he uses English more with non-native speakers.

- **P5** – the fifth participant was a 23-year-old student from Turkey. He has been learning English for ten years. His self-perceived level of English is B2. He agrees that English is a modern *lingua franca* and claims that he uses English with non-native speakers more.

- **P6** – the sixth participant was a 23-year-old student from Bulgaria. She has been learning English since kindergarten and claims to be on a B2 level. She knows Spanish on a C2 level as well. She agrees that English is a modern *lingua franca* and claims to use it more with non-native speakers.

As it can be seen, the sample that has been gathered is neither representative nor pretending to reach any research completeness. Our task, which must be emphasised, was only to investigate the tendencies of ELF users concerning the employment of communicative strategies and to indicate the frequency of use that would provide us with some basic information concerning their language choices.

3.3. Data collection

The data was collected with the help of an asynchronous structured online interview. The use of an asynchronous structured online interview was connected with the fact that such an instrument is very flexible in terms of small-scale research (Ratislavová & Ratislav, 2014). The questions in the interview were aimed to obtain information concerning participants' self-awareness in the use of communicative strategies, as they were asked if and how often they use a particular strategy. The questions were created in such a way to allow them to clearly understand what a given strategy requires, therefore, examples of use were provided. Additional issues concerning their general use of English in the *lingua franca* context were also discussed if they logically followed the direction of the conversation and the participants were eager to discuss them. A fixed time frame was established, where the participants had two weeks to fill in the interview, to allow us to respond to any misunderstandings or interesting issues that were raised by their answers.

4. Results

After the interviews were received, the answers were analysed and compared. The results are presented in two sections in the following way: (1) difficulties in ELF communicative exchanges and (2) use and frequency of employing communicative strategies by ELF users.

4.1. Difficulties in ELF communicative exchanges

All of the participants, when asked about communicative problems that they sometimes experience in *lingua franca* communication, answered that the problem of miscommunication is common. Among the reasons provided by them, vocabulary problems were indicated as the most common source of miscommunication, with the participants stating:

> "when I try to explain a situation with more complex vocabulary, I often realise I do not know how is the word" (P1).

> "when someone use more difficult words I usually have problems in understanding them" (P4).

When asked about their reaction to such situations, three of them indicated that they prefer to remain silent in such a situation:

> "If I know I will not be able to explain my idea I remain silent" (P1).

"yeah, I will stay quiet" (P4).

Two stated that they would either stay quiet or laugh nervously: "I prefer to remain silent and laugh because the other person can think I am stupid if I talk without knowing the topic" (P2). However, one of the responses showed a different attitude, as one participant said that he tries to deal with the problematic situation as he knows that: "I will have to deal with burdens sooner or later" (P5).

The subsequent cause of problems was the speed of delivering the message which sometimes poses real difficulties, not only in understanding the message but also in delivering one, as one participant stated that she often makes mistakes when talking too fast. Two of them also pointed to the problem of various accents which may be sometimes intelligible: "you have to get used to the different accents of people from different parts of the world because sometimes you can have listening problems" (P2).

What was quite interesting in the provided answers is that the participants seem to be fully aware of their own skills and the lack thereof. They stated that they are *afraid of* making a mistake, they do not want to be *laughed at*, and remaining *silent* is their best option if they experience difficulties. It can be connected with the fact that they are simply insecure in terms of their own skills, which they assess against the standard English, regardless of whether their attempts are successful – the message is delivered, understood and acted upon – but rather whether they were grammatically correct in doing so.

4.2. Frequency and use of communicative strategies by ELF users

The participants' answers concerning the frequency and use of communicative strategies by ELF users are divided into three groups: (1) avoidance or reduction strategies, (2) achievement or compensatory strategies, and (3) stalling or time gaining tactics, as exemplified in the theoretical part following Dörnyei's (1995) framework.

4.2.1. Avoidance or reduction strategies

In the area of avoidance or reduction strategies, the participants claimed that they often remain silent if the subject matter is too difficult or they lack ample knowledge to deal with the topic. One of the participants claimed that she is more eager to involve herself in the conversation of difficult topics if she knows her interlocutor well: " I avoid difficult topics only if I am not confident of another person" (P6), which means that it is easier to make an effort when you are not judged by your delivery. Other participants were in agreement that they do not talk with others when they feel that their skills are not appropriate: " I just feel that I am not good enough" (P4), "I can make a mistake when I don't know what I am talking about" (P5). It may imply that the use of avoidance strategies is common, but also constrained by the environment where the conversation takes place and the interlocutors themselves. The higher the level of familiarity with the environment and other interlocutors, the lower the possibility of avoidance seems to be. Moreover, the higher the feeling of anxiety concerning one's skills, the lower the chance of successful conversations is.

4.2.2. Achievement or compensation strategies

In the case of the strategy of circumlocution, the participants show a tendency towards the use of this strategy in case of having troubles with putting the message forward. All of them claim that they always or almost always try to provide the interlocutor with a general idea of what they want to put forward if they cannot recollect the proper word in a given context either in the form of a definition or by using exemplification. One of the participants claimed that the frequency of using definitions is closely related with the level of language that is required: "when the vocabulary requires a higher level I need to use definitions, I use them often" (P4). Another claimed that it is sometimes: "the only way to say what I want to say" (P6).

When asked whether they sometimes use words which only point towards the one they have in mind, yet are sometimes less precise, all of the participants claimed to do so, yet with varying intensity. One of the participants said: "yes,

I do, and almost always" (P2), whereas the rest said that they do it sometimes, with one participant stating that such a situation happens: "much often than I want, but usually it happens to me" (P1).

When asked about word-coinage, the participants stated that it happens rarely or never. Yet, if it happens they do not consider it a problem, but rather, as it was aptly stated by one of the participants: "a common mistake that arises in communication" (P2). However, in the question concerning the fact whether they foreignise their L1 words by, e.g. adding the *–ing* ending by saying *messaging* instead of *sending a text message,* the results show that the majority of them either rarely, not often or never foreignise mother-tongue words. They were not sure when and why does it occur, but two participants said that it is connected with the fact that some words 'look' similar in English and their native tongue, so sometimes they may:

"use [their] native vocabulary 'changed' into English" (P1).

"say the word in such a way that it sounds like English" (P6).

When it comes to the use of non-linguistic means the participants were unanimous in stating that they very often use gestures when talking. In case of using facial expressions and gestures, which are considered salient in any type of conversation not only in the context of ELF, the participants stated that:

"I use that kinds of action" (P1).

"sometimes your hands can be better than your words" (P5).

When the participants were asked about the possibility of translating word for word from their L1 to L2 (in this case English) while communicating, their answers showed lack of unanimity in the use of this particular strategy. The participants stated that they use it sometimes when they have problems finding the right word:

"It happens from time to time" (P1).

"I sometimes translate word for word, but sometimes I get it wrong" (P6).

One stated that it happens: "sometimes, but I try to avoid it, as it is not helpful" (P5) whereas the other stated that she never uses it as: "the language arises by itself" (P2), so he finds no reason for translations.

When it comes to code-switching, which is considered a common strategy while L2 is used as it helps to avoid prolonged silence and helps to put the message forward, the participants are not unanimous in the answers provided, however, four of them say that they use code-switching in order to communicate effectively:

> "Yes I do. Terms from Spanish to English look similar for me, so they use to coincide, in this way if I am not sure, I will use my native vocabulary 'changed' into English" (P1).

> "From time to time it happens. I will use a words in my L1 if I can't remember what English word can be used" (P4).

One participant showed a negative attitude towards such a statement: "if I am speaking in English I try to use English words" (P3) and one stated that he uses this strategy from time to time, yet remained undecided about the usefulness of it "It sometimes happens, but also sometimes it is ineffective" (P6).

The subsequent type of compensation strategies that were taken into consideration in the study considers the possibility of asking for lexical help or clarification when facing a language problem that slows down or causes the communicative exchange to stop.

They stated that they always or very often ask for clarification if they have problems with understanding what the other person is trying to say:

> "I always use such phrases: Could you repeat? I didn't understand that" (P1).

> "I ask the other person to explain what they mean" (P5).

and also try to do the same if they observe that their interlocutor does not understand them.

> "If someone does not understand me I try to explain the fact in a different way. I also repeat the message because maybe the receiver did not fully understand" (P4).

> "I try to explain if I see that someone does not understand me, but usually I just repeat myself" (P5).

The results gathered allow us to state that ELF users have a rather strong tendency to ask for clarification or use other forms of lexical help in order to put the message forward with all respondents agreeing and strongly agreeing with the statements provided in the questionnaire.

4.2.3. Stalling or time gaining tactics

In the category of using time gaining tactics, the results gathered yield a quite interesting set of answers, especially in the area of using filled pauses. The majority of the participants (P1; P2; P3; P5; P6) use filled pauses such as *errr*, *uhmm*, *so*, in the form of time gaining tactics, yet some consider the use of them as an example of poor language skills.

> "Yes, I sometimes use them, but I think its not good to do it" (P2).

> "When I use them I feel that the other person thinks that I am not a good speaker" (P3).

One participant (P4) stated that he likes to think silently and does not use filled pauses. It seems, therefore, that the tactic is considered by them as effective, yet should not be used as it is connected with having lower language knowledge.

In regard to the use of such phrases as *let me think; Oh, just give me a minute; well...*, *as* the participants claim that they sometimes use them but they try not to overuse them.

> "I will sometimes say something like that, when I am trying to remember the word I need, but usually I can't" (P3).

> "I try to be clear when I talk in English, but sometimes I need some time to think, so I say something like that to have some extra time. But I don't do it often" (P5).

With one participant (P2) stating that she does not use such phrases but prefers filled pauses, it may be therefore stated that stalling or time-gaining tactics are used by the participants, but they are not used as often as expected.

5. Discussion

The results showed rather small differences among the results which seem to corroborate the hypothesis that ELF users use various communicative strategies in their utterances. What can be observed, however, is that certain preferences are slightly less favoured by the users of ELF. It seems that those strategies that require manipulation of the language content and adjusting the language forms to meet the goals of communication (transformations, paraphrases, foreignisation, and coining new words) are less frequently used; whereas those which are more limited, namely using options that are still placed within the confines of a given language and do not require changes of the forms or structures being used (circumlocution, approximation, generalisation, code-switching, asking for help, and time gaining tactics with body language being the most popular among them) are more commonly observed. This seems to be a possible direction in introducing communicative strategies if ELF is to be taught. What can be also noted is that avoidance strategies are also commonly used by the participants of the study. Contrary to the findings made by Pitzl (2005) that ELF users show high levels of involvement and cooperation in a communicative exchange, and also to what was claimed by Mauranen (2006) in the research on pro-active behaviour, the presented case study yields a slightly different result. ELF users use avoidance strategies almost as often as compensation ones.

Among the most common problems, the pace of delivery of the message, intelligible accent, or difficult vocabulary were enlisted. It seems that the preparation of students to communication in English as a foreign language is not enough to prepare them to deal with the unpredictable nature of ELF communicative exchanges. Preparing the students to one pronunciation model leads to a situation where an understanding of other, international models is harder. Not enough communicative practice leads to problems with fluency. And a problem with fluency, in turn, results in an increased use of avoidance strategies. Interestingly enough, there is no correlation between the answers to the questions and the linguistic backgrounds of the learners as the answers given were not in a line with the user's language level, the length of learning of the language, and whether they are bilingual or multilingual.

6. Limitations of the study

It has to be noted that the present study has limitations. The limitations are due to the fact that the gathered sample consisting of six participants was the only one available in the environment of the researcher that would meet the definition of a *lingua franca* user. Given the limited size of the sample, it was not possible to draw inferences of statistical significance from the results. The idea was not to establish any pattern statistically, but simply to get some indication of whether typical ELF users use communicative strategies and whether a certain preference towards a given type is observable.

7. Conclusion

The use of various communicative strategies is mainly aimed at having a successful communicative exchange among the interlocutors. Various studies concerning the usefulness of training learners in the use of communicative strategies, such as those of O'Malley and Chamot (1990), Dörnyei (1995), as well as those of Cohen (2002), Nakatani (2005), Maleki (2007), Thomas and McDonagh (2013), and Kongsom (2016) concerning the effectiveness of communicative strategies when used in L2 exchanges, showed that explicit training and the active use of communicative strategy help the learners deal with communication more successfully in comparison to those people who do not receive such training or do not employ such strategies; proficient language users that employ communicative strategies show a far greater ability in moulding the language to their needs and show a stronger inclination towards sustaining communication regardless of the possible inadequacies in their language proficiency. In light of the research on the use of strategies in ELF, it seems plausible to assume that effective use of communicative strategies is one of the most crucial elements of having a successful communication in the *lingua franca* context due to its extreme fluidity and variation. However, what was revealed in Vettorel's (2018) study was that the importance of communicative strategies in ELF has not yet been recognised in ELT materials. Therefore, a more open attitude of educators towards introducing the knowledge concerning the nature of ELF and what follows (understanding the need of incorporating such knowledge into the teaching programmes with an emphasis on training the learners to effectively use communicative strategies) is advisable. However, more research is needed which would exceed the scope of this paper, so the self-reported use of strategies. As the study of Tan et al. (2012) revealed, there may be discrepancies between the self-reported and actual use of strategies by the English users, so observation of ELF learners along with self-reported interviews on a bigger scale seems to be advisable in future research.

References

Białystok, E. (1990). *Communication strategies*. Blackwell
Böhringer, H. (2007). *The sound of silence: silent and filled pauses in English as a lingua franca business interaction*. Unpublished MA thesis. The University of Vienna.

Breiteneder, A. (2005). The naturalness of English as a European lingua franca: the case of the 'third person –s'. *Vienna English Working Papers, 14*(2), 3-26.

Choi, K., & Jeon, Y. J. (2016). Suggestion on teachers' beliefs research on teaching English as a lingua franca. *Paper presented at the 2016 International Conference on Platform Technology and Service (PlatCon), Jeju, South Korea* (pp. 1-4). https://doi.org/10.1109/PlatCon.2016.7456828

Cogo, A. (2009). Accommodating difference in ELF conversations: a study of pragmatic strategies. In A. Mauranen (Ed.), *English as a lingua franca: studies and findings* (pp. 254-273). Cambridge Scholars Publishing.

Cogo, A., & Dewey, M. (2006). Efficiency in ELF communication: from pragmatic motives to lexico-grammatical innovation. *The Nordic Journal of English Studies, 5*(2), 59-93.

Cohen, A. D. (2002). Assessing and enhancing language learners' strategies. *Hebrew Higher Education, 10,* 1-11.

Corder, S. P. (1981). *Error analysis and interlanguage.* Oxford University Press.

Dewey, M. (2006). *English as a lingua franca: an empirical study of innovation in lexis and grammar.* Unpublished PhD thesis. King's College London.

Dimoski, B.,Yujobo, Y. J., & Imai, M. (2016). Exploring the effectiveness of communicative strategies through pro-active listening in ELF-informed pedagogy. *Language Education in Asia, 7*(2), 67-87. https://camtesol.org/Download/LEiA_V7_I2_2016/LEiA_V7I2A02_Dimoski_Yujobo_Imai.pdf

Dobao, A. M. F., & Martínez, I. M. P. (2007). Negotiating meaning in interaction between English and Spanish speakers via communicative strategies. *Atlantis, 29*(1), 87-105.

Dörnyei, Z. (1995). On the teachability of communication strategies. *TESOL Quarterly,* 29(1), 55-85. https://doi.org/10.2307/3587805

Færch, C., & Kasper, G. (1983). *Strategies in interlanguage communication.* Longman.

Gu, Y. (2012). Learning strategies: prototypical core and dimensions of variation. *Studies in Self-Access Learning Journal, 3*(4), 330-356.

Horváthová, B. (2013). *Language learning strategies in listening comprehension.* ASPA.

Hülmbauer, C. (2013). From within and without: the virtual and the plurilingual in ELF. *Journal of English as a Lingua Franca, 2*(1), 47-73. https://doi.org/10.1515/jelf-2013-0003

Hülmbauer, C., Böhringer, H., & Seidlhofer, B. (2008). Introducing English as a lingua franca (ELF): precursor and partner in intercultural communication. *Synergies Europe, 3,* 25-36. https://gerflint.fr/Base/Europe3/hulmbauer.pdf

Jenkins, J. (2000). *English as a lingua franca: attitude and identity.* Oxford University Press.

Klimpfinger, T. (2007). 'Mind you sometimes you have to mix' – the role of code-switching in English as a lingua franca. *Vienna English Working Papers, 16*(2), 36-61.

Kongsom, T. (2016). The impact of teaching communication strategies on English speaking of engineering undergraduates. *PASAA, 51,* 39-69.

Lichtkoppler, J. (2007). 'Male. Male.' - 'Male?' - 'The sex is male' - The role of repetition in English as a lingua franca conversations. *VIEWS, 16*(1), 39-65.

Llurda, E., Bayyurt, Y., & Sifakis, N. (2018). Raising teachers' awareness about English and English as a lingua franca. In P. Garret & J. Cotts (Eds), The Routledge handbook of language awareness. Routledge.

Lopriore, L., & Vettorel, P. (2016). A shift in ELT perspective: world Englishes and ELF in the EFL classroom. In N. Tsantila, J. Mandalios & M. Ilkos (Eds), *ELF: pedagogical and interdisciplinary perspectives* (pp. 8-15). Deree –The American College of Greece.

Macaro, E. (2006). Strategies for language learning and use: revisiting the theoretical framework. *Modern Language Journal, 90*(3), 320-337. https://doi.org/10.1111/j.1540-4781.2006.00425.x

Maleki, A. (2007). Teachability of communication strategies: an Iranian experience. *System, 35*(4), 583-594. https://doi.org/10.1016/j.system.2007.04.001

Maley, A. (2009). ELF: a teacher's perspective. *Language and intercultural communication, 9*(3), 187-200. https://doi.org/10.1080/14708470902748848

Mauranen, A. (2006). Signaling and preventing misunderstanding in ELF communication. *International Journal of the Sociology of Language, 177,* 123-150.

Nakatani, V. (2005). The effects of awareness-raising training on oral communication strategy use. *The Modern Language Journal, 89*(1), 76-91.

O'Malley, M., & Chamot, A. (1990). *Learning strategies in second language acquisition.* Cambridge University Press. https://doi.org/10.1017/CBO9781139524490

Pavlenko, A. (2002). Poststructuralist approaches to the study of social factors in second language leaning and use. In V. Cook (Ed.), Portraits of the L2 user (pp. 277-302). Multilingual Matters.

Phillipson, R. (1992). *Linguistic imperialism.* Oxford University Press.

Pitzl, M. L. (2005). Non-understanding in English as a lingua franca: examples from a business context. *Vienna English Working Papers, 14*(2), 50-71.

Rabab'ah, G. (2015). The effect of communication strategy training on the development of EFL learners' strategic competence and oral communicative ability. *Journal of Psycholinguistic Research, 45*(3), 625-651. https://doi.org/10.1007/s10936-015-9365-3

Ratislavová, K., & Ratislav, J. (2014). Asynchronous email interview as a qualitative research method in the humanities. *Human Affairs, 24*(4), 452-460. https://doi.org/10.2478/s13374-014-0240-y

Richards, J. C., Platt, J., & Weber, H. (1985). *Longman dictionary of applied linguistics.* Longman.

Richards, J., & Rodgers, T. (2001). *Approaches and methods in language teaching.* Cambridge University Press.

Scarcella, R., & Oxford, R. (1992). *The tapestry of language learning: the individual in the communicative classroom.* Heinle & Heinle.

Seidlhofer, B. (2001). Closing the conceptual gap: the case for a description of English as a lingua franca. *International Journal of Applied Linguistics, 11*(2), 133-158. https://doi.org/10.1111/1473-4192.00011

Seidlhofer, B. (2005). Language variation and change: the case of English as a lingua franca. In K. Dziubalska-Kolaczyk & J. Przedlacka (Eds), *English pronunciation models: a changing scene* (pp. 59-75). Peter Lang.

Tan, K. H., Fariza, N., & Jaradat, M. N. (2012). Communication strategies among EFL students – an examination of frequency of use and types of strategies used. *GEMA Online Journal of Language Studies, 12*, 831-848.

Tarone, E. (1977). Some thoughts on the notion of "communication strategies". In C. Færch & G. Kasper (Eds), Strategies in interlanguage communication (pp. 61-74). Longman.

Terrel, T. (1977). A natural approach to second language acquisition and learning. *Modern Language Journal, 61*(1), 325-37. https://doi.org/10.2307/324551

Thomas, J., & McDonagh, D. (2013). Shared language: towards more effective communication. *The Australasian Medical Journal, 6*(1), 46-54.

Turula, A. (2010). *Teaching English as a foreign language. From theory to practice and all the way back.* Wydawnictwo Wyższej Szkoły Lingwistycznej.

Váradi, T. (1980). Notes and discussion. Strategies of target language learner communication: message–adjustment. *IRAL - International Review of Applied Linguistics in Language Teaching, 18*(1-4), 59-71. https://doi.org/10.1515/iral.1980.18.1-4.59

Vettorel, P. (2018). ELF and communication strategies: are they taken into account in ELT materials? *RELC Journal, 49*(1), 58-73. https://doi.org/10.1177/0033688217746204

Watterson, M. (2008). Repair of non-understanding in English in international communication. *World Englishes, 27*(3/4), 378-406. https://doi.org/10.1111/j.1467-971X.2008.00574.x

3 Acquisition of Japanese through translation

Kinji Ito[1] and Shannon M. Hilliker[2]

Abstract

Acquiring and retaining vocabulary knowledge are two of the most important aspects of second language (L2) learning. Some scholars (e.g. Hedrick, Harmom, & Linerode, 2004; Nation, 1999; Stone & Urquhart, 2008) advocate that we should re-think and explore in depth the importance of vocabulary. According to Wilkins (1972), "while without grammar very little can be conveyed, without vocabulary *nothing* can be conveyed" (p. 111). In other words, vocabulary is the foundation of language because without sufficient vocabulary knowledge L2 learners will not be able to express themselves satisfactorily or comprehend incoming information. Vocabulary items are thus the basic building blocks of language (Read, 2001) and their acquisition naturally leads to more efficient communication. Since, in today's academic settings, language courses are designed to develop learners' communicative competencies, translation has been overlooked. Accordingly, the study that will be presented had a total of 21 participants who took the course *Japanese Through Translation* designed for intermediate Japanese language learners during the 2016-2017 academic year at a public university in the United States. Participants took two different types of vocabulary quizzes which had a variety of lexical items they learned throughout the semester. This study examined two different ways of learning vocabulary – deliberate and incidental – one through communication and the other through translation, respectively. The results indicated that most of the words learners retained were those

1. University of Pennsylvania, Philadelphia, Pennsylvania, United States; kinji110@gmail.com

2. Binghamton University, Binghamton, New York, United States; hilliker@binghamton.edu

How to cite this chapter: Ito, K., & Hilliker, S. M. (2019). Acquisition of Japanese through translation. In B. Loranc-Paszylk (Ed.), *Rethinking directions in language learning and teaching at university level* (pp. 53-74). Research-publishing.net. https://doi.org/10.14705/rpnet.2019.31.891

Chapter 3

which had been taught by means of translation. Hence, it can be said that translation has a positive impact on the acquisition of vocabulary because learners have a better chance of coming across more lexicons/words when they are engaged in translation tasks. Although the role of translation in language pedagogy has still been underappreciated due to negative associations with the antiquated grammar-translation method, it is time to reconsider its effectiveness for L2 learning.

Keywords: cognitive processes, incidental learning, Japanese, translation, vocabulary acquisition.

1. Introduction

The role of translation in language pedagogy has been overlooked and underappreciated, not only in academic settings, but also in the real world due to negative associations with the grammar-translation method used over half a century ago. As the name of this method indicates, the main focus is on specific grammar rules and vocabulary words embedded in various reading passages, and in translating them. It has been said that in this method no attempt is made to develop communicative competences such as speaking and listening comprehension (Lems, Miller, & Soro, 2010). In the past, scholars (e.g. Duff, 1989; Sankey, 1991; Wilkins, 1974) have been against the use of translation as a language learning tool, and thus "argued that translation is not a useful tool when acquiring a second or foreign language [because] it provides a simplistic one-to-one [correspondence] between the [source and the target] language [which] can cause interference between them" (Fernández-Guerra, 2014, p. 153). Moreover, it has been claimed that translation is just an artificial exercise that has nothing to do with a communicative approach to language teaching (Fernández-Guerra, 2014). Researchers in the field of translation studies have also affirmed that this is probably one of the reasons why translation has been overlooked. Dagilienė (2012) states that translation is still ignored as a useful language learning tool to date due to the fact that the anti-translation side continues to believe that it is not a communicative activity.

As mentioned in Fernández-Guerra (2014), "[r]ecent studies, however, show that far from being useless, translation can be a great aid to foreign language learning" (p. 153). For example, researchers have demonstrated that translation has a positive impact on the acquisition of vocabulary, and that learning vocabulary through translation is effective because learners have a better chance of coming across more lexicons/words when translating. One study group (Barletta, Klingner, & Orosco, 2011) examined two different ways of learning vocabulary, one through translation and the other through communication (i.e. oral activity). The results indicated that most of the words learners retained were those which had been taught by means of translation exercises. Today, translation can be one of the most useful techniques, especially for those learning a second or foreign language, in our present globalised world. Moreover, because translation has been defined as "the process of changing something that is written or spoken into another language" (Stevenson, 2010, p. 1899), it is conceivable that translation actually does have something to do with communicative approaches to language teaching.

Therefore, to add to the growing body of studies on the benefits of translation in language learning, the purpose of this study was to assess students' vocabulary development by means of translation tasks. This study has important results as a focus on vocabulary learning in the field of translation is missing. Learners have access to unknown lexicons/words when translating. Thus, the efficacy of learning vocabulary through translation and communication was also investigated.

2. Literature review

2.1. Interconnections between translation and vocabulary learning

Since translation is the process of changing something spoken or written into another language, it has been closely linked with linguistics. In order to create refined products, it has been said that translators should be familiar with both source and target cultures and languages, and have the ability to express thoughts clearly and concisely in both languages. Furthermore, many studies (e.g. Christopher, 2012; Jackson, 2014; Sofer, 2005) observe that because "meaning transfer is the translator's most clearly defined task" (Guzmán, 2010, p. 18) it is important for translators to possess extensive vocabulary knowledge in both languages.

According to Ur (2012), language learners need to recognise that there are several aspects of vocabulary knowledge including form, spelling, etc. She goes on to explain how important meaning is to vocabulary learning as follows:

> "The meaning of a word or expression is what it refers to, or denotes, in the real world. This is given in dictionaries as its definition. Occasionally a lexical item in English has no parallel in the learners' L1, and you will find yourself explaining an actual concept as well as the item that represents it" (Ur, 2012, p. 61).

Interestingly, Wilkins (1972) unequivocally asserts that "while without grammar very little can be conveyed, without vocabulary *nothing* can be conveyed" (p. 111). It is clear that vocabulary is the foundation of language; therefore, in order to achieve their respective goals, vocabulary knowledge is not only vital for language learners, but also translators. In short, translation is useful for acquiring lexical knowledge, and vocabulary is one of the integral elements of language. Therefore, it can be said that translation is beneficial for language learning if used appropriately. However, translation has been neglected for years because the anti-translation side has argued that translation is mostly regarded as a skill which does not directly link with the other four competencies, and thus should not be used in L2 teaching (Zojer, 2009).

2.2. Procedures of vocabulary learning

Some scholars (e.g. Anderson & Freebody, 1981; Hedrick et al., 2004; Nation, 1999; Stone & Urquhart, 2008) advocate that we should re-think and explore in depth the importance of vocabulary. In other words, vocabulary is the foundation of language because without sufficient vocabulary knowledge L2 learners will not be able to express themselves satisfactorily or comprehend incoming information. Vocabulary items are thus the basic building blocks of language (Read, 2001) and their acquisition naturally leads to more efficient communication.

Hadley (1993) mentions that while native speakers of English possess vocabularies of 10,000-100,000 words, L2 learners of English typically have between 2,000-7,000 words when they start their post-secondary education. Since vocabulary acquisition is an incremental process, this can also be applied to learners of other languages. Kruidenier (2002) suggests that it is important for L2 learners to learn the meaning of new vocabulary items in context. Thus, it is essential to be exposed to a wide range of contextualised vocabulary. Interestingly, according to Whyatt (2009), such exposure in the context of translation tasks is naturally linked with the need to actively manipulate vocabulary. Moreover, from a teacher's perspective, it is said that since lexical knowledge including style, tone, connotations, etc., is difficult to teach explicitly in the classroom, translation is highly effective for developing vocabulary knowledge.

Ur (2012) states that there are two procedures for vocabulary learning: deliberate and incidental. Since the former is instructional while the latter is accidental, they are also called explicit and implicit vocabulary learning, respectively (Klapper, 2008). More specifically, the former refers to situations in which vocabulary items that are typically found in textbooks designed for foreign language courses are intentionally provided to learners for review to expand their lexical knowledge. The latter, on the other hand, applies to situations in which learners happen to encounter unknown vocabulary items through reading, listening, translation, etc. Therefore, the main difference between these procedures is whether intentionality is involved. However, as Laufer and Nation (2013) have observed, "the experimental and observational study of both deliberate and incidental vocabulary learning activities is a much neglected area of vocabulary studies" (p. 172). In a similar way, Taylor (1990) has claimed that even though vocabulary acquisition has been an undervalued area for quite some time now, it is essential for language mastery. The present study hinges on the distinction between deliberate and incidental learning, particularly significant to the acquisition of lexical items, and thus attempts to identify the differences in effect of vocabulary retention between them.

Nation (2003) claims that deliberate learning in conjunction with opportunities for learning through communication is far more effective because it can result in a large amount of knowledge that is retained over substantial periods of time. In contrast, Krashen (1989) argues that language is subconsciously acquired and learners do not know exactly what they are acquiring. He goes on to assert that conscious attention is concerned with message, not form; therefore, the acquisition process of linguistic knowledge is identical to what has been termed 'incidental learning'. The dichotomy between both learning procedures is indeed a dilemma. With vocabulary learning, the former involves the way in which language learners memorise item after item by referring to their respective translation equivalents from vocabulary lists. Thus, although intentional learning is quick since it does not require the use of a dictionary, it is in a sense superficial because learners may not be able to use learned knowledge properly in context. In contrast, incidental learning involves learners coming across unknown items during target language activities such as reading and learning their usage in context. Even if it takes time to look them up in a dictionary, such physical action that engages cognitive processes will help learners retain knowledge better in their memory system. Therefore, when it comes to learning vocabulary, it is conceivable that combining these two procedures may be the ideal. As Ur (2012) states, "most researchers agree that we need to include some deliberate, focused vocabulary-teaching procedures as a supplement to – though not a substitute for – incidental acquisition through extensive reading and listening" (p. 65).

Other researchers (e.g. Cobb & Horst, 2004; Ellis, 2008; Hill & Laufer, 2003) also point out that incidental learning alone is not sufficient for the acquisition of L2 vocabulary items, and thus needs to be supplemented by explicit learning. Huckin and Coady (1999), on the other hand, suggest that as "a by-product of the main cognitive activity" (p. 182) incidental acquisition is the primary means by which L2 learners develop their vocabulary knowledge beyond the first few thousand most common words which are usually acquired explicitly (i.e. deliberately). They also observe, however, that incidental vocabulary learning is still not fully understood, and that many questions are still unanswered.

2.3. Case studies of vocabulary learning strategies

As discussed in the previous section, the study of deliberate and incidental lexical learning activities is a neglected area. However, there have been few studies on the effects of each procedure conducted in the past. For example, Tabrizi and Feiz (2016) examined the effect of deliberate and incidental vocabulary learning strategies on Iranian high school students learning English. A total of 50 participants were randomly divided into two groups: one experimental group with 25 students using flashcards, and a second experimental group with 25 students using textual-pictorial glosses. A pretest composed of vocabulary items in multiple-choice format was administered in order to determine their pre-existing lexical knowledge. According to their findings, both groups were at almost the same level and thus the researchers concluded that there was no significant difference between them.

On completion of the three sessions, a posttest was administered in the same format as the pretest and included the new vocabulary items. Tabrizi and Feiz (2016) found that there was a significant difference between the groups. The deliberate group outperformed the incidental group by a large margin. The researchers account for this outcome by noting that deliberate learning is more focussed and goal-oriented than incidental learning.

In another case study, Ahmad (2011) conducted research on 20 Saudi English learners regarding the relative efficacy of deliberate and incidental vocabulary learning processes. His main goal was to compare the impact of direct learning on the acquisition of new vocabulary items with that of the incidental approach of guessing the meanings of new words via contextual clues. Ahmad concludes that the incidental vocabulary technique can be a good method for both teaching and learning vocabulary items because it helps learners develop reading comprehension and promotes lexical acquisition.

Chapter 3

On the one hand, other researchers (e.g. Huckin & Coady, 1999; Krashen, 1989; Nagy, Herman, & Anderson, 1985) who have noted the effectiveness of incidental learning explain that language learners acquire more vocabulary knowledge through extensive reading and guessing the meaning of unfamiliar words. They further note that a large portion of the vocabulary children learn in L1 is incidental. On the other hand, some scholars (e.g. Elgort, 2011; Hulstijn, 2003; Nation, 2001; Schmitt, 2010) have claimed that experiments involving deliberate learning indicate that acquisition and long-term retention rates are better than those of incidental learning. In either case, what is important here is whether or not such information can be retained in the memory system for future use. However, according to one study group (Ornstein, 1992), the implications of the distinction between deliberate and incidental approaches for understanding memory retention remain unclear. Moreover, a number of studies (e.g. Braun & Rubin, 1998; Shahpari & Shamshiri, 2014; Zandieh & Jafarigohar, 2012) have found that there was no significant difference in vocabulary retention between deliberate and incidental learning techniques.

2.4. Gaps in the literature: research on translation and vocabulary learning

In order to explore which approach/process works better for L2 learners, past studies have examined the differences between deliberate and incidental vocabulary learning. It is problematic that the participants in all of the above-mentioned studies were divided into groups in which they only went through designated tasks once. The outcomes achieved by the deliberate learning group were juxtaposed with the incidental learning group. Researchers formed these groups based on pretests or language level proficiency tests given prior to the experiments. That is, it was assumed that both groups were formed neutrally. Nevertheless, what was disregarded was that these tests only administered one time were insufficient to accurately evaluate the subjects' proficiency levels, and thus apt to be biased unless they were grouped based on the result of multiple tests. Therefore, instead of classifying them into different experimental categories, researchers could have each subject participating in their research go through both steps/phases of the overall process: deliberate and incidental learning.

2.5. Research question and hypothesis

There are mainly two sets of ways of encountering new vocabulary items (i.e. lexis). The first is when learners are outside the classroom and engaged in reading a book, watching a movie, listening to music, etc. Another is when they are in the classroom in which new items are introduced orally and/or visually by the teacher or are recognised by themselves through activities such as reading a text or doing a translation task. This study focusses on the latter as this research was conducted in the classroom, and will therefore address the following Research Question (RQ) and Hypothesis (H):

> RQ: Does learning vocabulary through incidental translation help learners retain knowledge better than learning vocabulary through deliberate oral instruction (i.e. communication)?

> H: Learning vocabulary through translation will outperform learning vocabulary through oral instruction. Unlike receiving vocabulary orally and visually, vocabulary encountered when working with translation materials will elicit the looking up of unknown items in their online dictionary, and this in turn will facilitate comprehension, memory consolidation, retention, and so forth.

3. Method

3.1. Participants

This is a classroom-based study which was conducted during the 2016-2017 academic year at a public university in the United States under the course name *Japanese Through Translation* designed for intermediate Japanese language learners. Twenty-one (nine female and 12 male) undergraduate students (ages

Chapter 3

ranging from 18 to 22) studying at an intermediate level took part in this research project. The only prerequisite for this course was that participants must have taken at least two semesters of college-level Japanese or had equivalent experience, and their native languages were English (16), Chinese (4), and Korean (1).

3.2. Design and procedure

The purpose of the study using the following procedure was to determine which approach best helps participants develop vocabulary knowledge and retention. Participants were required to bring a dictionary (hardcopy, electronic, online, etc.) to class. They could use it to look up unfamiliar words anytime they encountered them in order to complete the given tasks, except during vocabulary quizzes.

3.2.1. Step 1

Throughout the semester, a variety of vocabulary was introduced to participants through both translation and communication. The former means that they encountered unfamiliar vocabulary during the given translation task as part of interactive classroom activities and had to use a dictionary in order to complete the translation. The latter means that, as in a traditional language classroom, the instructor orally introduced new vocabulary items by using the blackboard or PowerPoint.

3.2.2. Step 2

At a later date, participants took two vocabulary quizzes in succession (the quizzes were composed of an equal number of vocabulary items learned through both methods).

In order to assess participants' spontaneous knowledge learned through both methods, quizzes were unannounced to the students. The contents of both quizzes were identical, but formats were different. The first one was composed of 'fill in the blank' questions, and the second one consisted of 'multiple choice' questions. Figure 1 and Figure 2 are quiz question examples.

Figure 1. Fill in the blank

Please translate the following into Japanese.
Context   Repetition   Omit   Theory   Depression
_____   _____   _____   _____   _____

Figure 2. Multiple choice

Please choose the most appropriate translation for each item from the table below.
Context   Repetition   Omit   Theory   Depression
_____   _____   _____   _____   _____
てんしゃ   りろん   はぶく   つうやく   いみ
せいしょ   ぶんみゃく   うつ   こうかん   くりかえし

The reason for the use of different types of format is to investigate whether there is a significant difference between the formats as follows:

- test a class on vocabulary knowledge without a clue through 'fill in the blank' formats, and

- test a class on vocabulary knowledge with a clue through 'multiple choice' formats.

It is hypothesised that this is how the actual effects of acquiring lexical items through both methods and ideas regarding their relationship with cognitive processes are discovered. Although the quizzes were also a small part of the participants' grade, since this study values studious effort, it was later announced that students were allowed to drop one of them (i.e. keep the better one) in compensation for not announcing they were having a quiz and therefore not having the ability to study.

4. Results and discussion

The present study had all the participants take two vocabulary quizzes in two formats: 'fill in the blank' and 'multiple choice'. Each format contained a total of 20 questions consisting of two sets of ten questions from each learning method: oral and translation. The contents of both quizzes were identical. The aim was to examine which format would better help them retrieve vocabulary knowledge from their memory systems, and to observe which method worked better for L2 learners. Table 1 is showcasing the results obtained from the quizzes. This will be followed by Table 2 displaying its statistical data.

Table 1. Results of the vocabulary quizzes[3]

Format	Fill in the blank		Multiple choice	
Method	Oral	Translation	Oral	Translation
P 1	7	9.5	1	8
P 2	6.5	8.5	4	10
P 3	5	7	4	6
P 4	4	8	5	7
P 5	0	2	3	6
P 6	8	10	10	10
P 7	9.5	7.5	3	8
P 8	2	3.5	6	10
P 9	4	4	2	7
P 10	4	8	7	10
P 11	2	6	4	7
P 12	4.5	4	3	5
P 13	3	9	8	10
P 14	3	6	3	8
P 15	4	3	5	10
P 16	0	0	2	4
P 17	3	5	5	8
P 18	6	4	6	6
P 19	2	5	5	6
P 20	3.5	5.5	2	5
P 21	3.5	6.5	7	10
TOTAL	84.5	122	95	161

3. In the table, all calculations were performed by ANOVA

There are four conditions: two different formats for two different methods. Therefore, the study adopted another statistical data analysis procedure called analysis of variance (ANOVA) using Statistical Package for the Social Sciences (SPSS) statistics and utilised one of the designs called repeated measures which allows one to compare three or more group means when participants are the same for each group. The results are as follows.

Table 2. Report generated by one-way ANOVA with repeated measures for vocabulary

Descriptive statistics

	N	M	SD
Oral/Fill	21	4.02	2.39
Translation/Fill	21	5.81	2.61
Oral/Multiple	21	4.52	2.25
Translation/Multiple	21	7.67	1.98

Tests of within-subjects effects

Source	df	F	Sig.
Type Greenhouse-Geisser	2.226	18.338	.000
Error (Type) Greenhouse-Geisser	44.520		

4.1. Analysing research question

According to the data called the *Descriptive statistic* given in Table 2, the calculated means for each format and method are graphed below (Figure 3).

For each format, the participants performed better with translation. As proof, according to the Greenhouse-Geisser given in Table 2, there was a statistically significant difference between the methods ($F(3, 80)=18.338$, $p<.05$). However, this only tells us the overall significance. Therefore, we need to look at the pairwise comparisons given in the same table presenting the outcomes of the Bonferroni post-hoc test. As shown in Table 3, this provides the significance level for differences between each format and method.

Figure 3. Means for each format and method

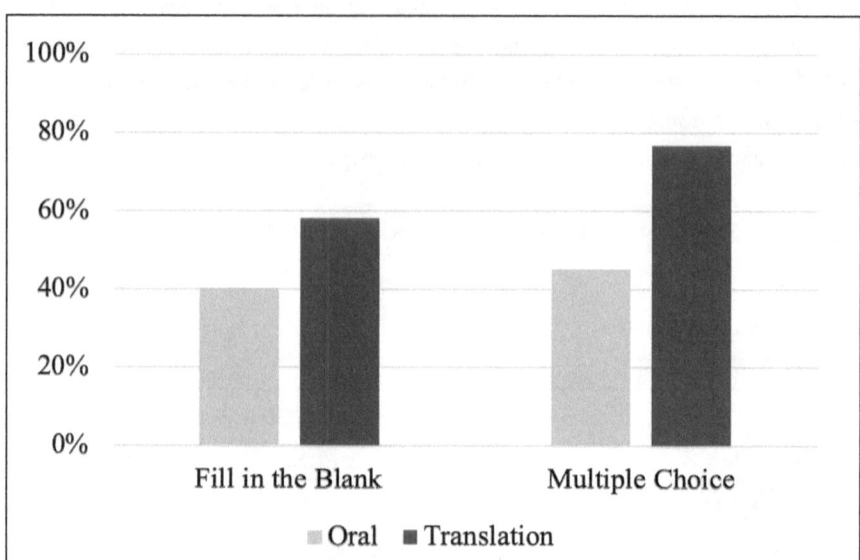

Table 3. Results generated by the Bonferroni for vocabulary

(I) Method	(J) Method	Sig.
1 Fill/Oral	2 Fill/Trans	.005
	3 Multi/Oral	.999
	4 Multi/Trans	.000
2 Fill/Trans	1 Fill/Oral	.005
	3 Multi/Oral	.255
	4 Multi/Trans	.008
3 Multiple/Oral	1 Fill/Oral	.999
	2 Fill/Trans	.255
	4 Multi/Trans	.000
4 Multiple/Trans	1 Fill/Oral	.000
	2 Fill/Trans	.008
	3 Multi/Oral	.000

As mentioned earlier, when p-value is smaller than .05, there is a statistically significant difference between the two groups. Interestingly, any combination involving 4 (Multiple/Trans) shows there is a statistically significant difference.

That is, the participants did best on the 'multiple choice' format through the translation method. Even when juxtaposing both outcomes yielded by 'fill in the blank' format, it is clear that the translation method produced better results.

Regarding the translation method, we first consider why the 'multiple choice' format was superior. Given the fact that all of the questions were identical, the former must have enabled students to access the knowledge retained somewhere in their memory systems. But, as the mean scores are about 58% for 'fill in the blank' and about 77% for 'multiple choice', if there was a specific cue that triggered some kind of information, the participants were more likely able to produce the correct output. Although multiple choice requires only recognition and results seem predictable, comparing the different formats is not as crucial as comparing the outcomes achieved by the two methods: incidental translation and deliberate oral instruction. This is because the research intended to examine the latter, and thus the formats were simply employed to see if there is a significant difference between the two. As proof, as shown in the profile plot below (Figure 4) created by ANOVA, it can be said that regardless of the format the translation method outperformed the other in both cases. Moreover, there is no significant difference between the two formats in the oral method.

Figure 4.   Profile plot for vocabulary learning

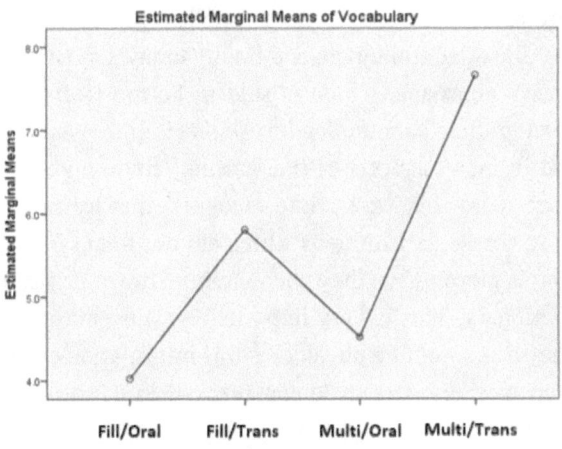

In the end, participants retained more lexical items learned through translation. Therefore, the hypothesis was supported. Kruidenier (2002) advocates that it is important for L2 learners to learn the meaning of new lexical items in context. Similarly, according to Whyatt (2009), such exposure in the context of translation tasks is certainly linked with the need to actively manipulate vocabulary. That is, incidental learning that involves learners coming across unknown items during target language activities such as translation and learning usage in context are highly effective for developing vocabulary knowledge.

5. Conclusion

The reason for investigating the efficacy of translation in academic settings is that it has heretofore been a largely neglected pedagogical approach. Language courses are typically designed to develop learners' language competencies in reading, listening, speaking, and writing, which have long been classified as core skills necessary for second language acquisition (Leow, 2015). In fact, however, in a broad sense, translation encompasses all of these basic skills since translation is defined as "the process of changing something that is written or spoken into another language" (Stevenson, 2010, p. 1899). Unfortunately, however, translation has been underappreciated due to its negative association with the grammar-translation method. This method was very popular a long time ago. Nevertheless, over time, it was gradually replaced with other teaching methods such as direct, audiolingual, and finally today's most popular method, the communicative approach, which is said to be most effective in helping L2 learners develop their communication skills (Lightbown & Spada, 2013). This is reflected in many aspects of the learning environments and teaching styles that we see today, but we have to recognise that learners have a better chance of coming across lexical items which are not found in textbooks when translating. What is more, when they encounter unknown items, they will look them up in a dictionary. This is very important because they are taking direct action, and if they do something physically, this information or knowledge will be stored in their memory system longer than when conventional classroom methods are employed.

As part of the effectiveness of translation, the study shed light on vocabulary acquisition. To reiterate, there are two procedures for vocabulary learning: deliberate and incidental. During the study, both procedures were employed as follows. For the former, lexical items were provided orally and visually in the classroom. For the latter, the participants used a dictionary when translating in order to complete the tasks given. Furthermore, there were two formats: 'fill in the blank' and 'multiple choice'. This was done to examine whether vocabulary learning was related to cognitive processing. The incidental procedure worked better for both formats, especially the latter. This suggests that lexical items learned through translation tend to be retained in the human memory systems longer and be recalled more easily when there is a specific cue. That is, using methods that entail some kind of deliberate physical action is a more effective way of learning vocabulary than traditional classroom approaches. In the case of this study, it was physical action that helped students retrieve learned information more efficiently.

Thelen and Lewandowska-Tomaszczyk (2010) state that "the translation process is a cognitive process in the first place" (p. 374) because there is constant transfer between source and target languages. Similarly, Sickinger (2017) claims that translation is firmly related to cognitive psychology and cognitive linguistics. As is well-known, the act of translation, including interpretation and transcription, is a practice that requires mental processes, decision-making, and the like. However, while translation practice is readily observable, cognitive activities are not. Therefore, mental processes of translation have been one of the main subjects in translation studies. This is part of the reason why this study examined how vocabulary learning took place. More specifically, this study discovered visible evidence that supports the efficacy of translation on vocabulary acquisition based on the fact that incidental vocabulary acquisition surpassed their opposing modes. It is now clear that acts of translation involving cognitive processes were more useful for storing information in and retrieving information from the memory system.

Traditionally, as referred to by many researchers (Dehn, 2008; Goldstein, 2014; Davey, Sterling, & Field, 2012) and as mentioned in Ito (2015, pp. 7-8), the most widely accepted and used model of information processing is the stage theory based on the work of Atkinson and Shiffrin (1968). The hypothesis is that when new information is taken in, it is manipulated in some way before it is stored (Lutz & Huitt, 2003). The stage theory model identifies three stages of memory: sensory memory, short-term or working memory, and long-term memory. This is also commonly referred to as the information processing model. Carter (2014) says that one of the best ways to develop vocabulary is to read and look up new words in the dictionary. This is the same process the participants in this study encountered when they engaged in translation tasks. Detecting or noticing unknown items initially comes through the sensory system, and the act of using a dictionary is the next step towards pushing them deeper into the memory system. Thereafter, if one wants to memorise the items s/he will write them down and practise using them to retain that knowledge in long-term memory. Hence, compared to oral instruction, which L2 learners might simply listen to in traditional classroom settings, the act of translation requires extensive vocabulary knowledge in order to complete tasks given. This supports the results that the participants retained more lexical items learned through translation involving cognitive processes.

In the future a study such as the one presented should be expanded to include different target languages and different levels of language acquisition in addition to a more focussed attention on cognitive processes.

References

Ahmad, J. (2011). Intentional vs. incidental vocabulary learning. *Interdisciplinary Journal of Contemporary Research in Business*, *3*(5), 67-75.

Anderson, R. C., & Freebody, P. (1981). Vocabulary knowledge. In J. Guthrie (Ed.), *Comprehension and teaching: research reviews* (pp. 77-117). International Reading Association.

Atkinson, R. C., & Shiffrin, R. M. (1968). Human memory: a proposed system and its control processes. In K. W. Spence & J. T. Spence (Eds), The psychology of learning and motivation (vol 2). Academic Press.

Barletta, L. M., Klingner, K., & Orosco, M. J. (2011). Writing acquisition among English language learners in U.S. schools. In Y. Durgunoglu & C. Goldenberg (Eds), *Language and literary development in bilingual settings* (pp. 210-244). The Guilfold Press.

Braun, K. A., & Rubin, D. C. (1998). A retrieval model of the spacing effect. *Memory, 6*(1), 37-65.

Carter, C. E. (2014). *Mindscapes: critical reading skills and strategies*. Wadsworth, Cengage Learning.

Christopher, E. M. (2012). *International management: explorations across cultures*. Kogan Page.

Cobb, T., & Horst, M. (2004). Is there an academic word list in French? In P. Bogaards & B. Laufer (Eds), *Vocabulary in a second language* (pp. 15-38). Benjamins. https://doi.org/10.1075/lllt.10.04cob

Dagilienė, I. (2012). Translation as a learning method in English language teaching. *Studies about Languages, 21*, 124-129.

Davey, G., Sterling, C., & Field, A. (2012). *Complete psychology*. Routledge.

Dehn, M. J. (2008). *Working memory and academic learning: assessment and intervention*. John Wiley & Sons, Inc.

Duff, A. (1989). *Translation*. Oxford University Press.

Elgort, I. (2011). Deliberate learning and vocabulary acquisition in a second language. *Language Learning, 61*(2), 367-413. https://doi.org/10.1111/j.1467-9922.2010.00613.x

Ellis, N. C. (2008). Usage-based and form-focused language acquisition. In P. Robinson & N. C. Ellis (Eds), *Handbook of cognitive linguistics and second language acquisition* (pp. 372-405). Routledge.

Fernández-Guerra, A. B. (2014). The usefulness of translation in foreign language learning: students' attitudes. *IJ-ELTS, 2*(1), 153-170.

Goldstein, E. (2014). *Cognitive psychology: connecting mind, research and everyday experience*. Thomson Higher Education.

Guzmán, M. C. (2010). *Gregory Rabassa's Latin American literature: a translator's visible legacy*. Bucknell University Press.

Hadley, A. O. (1993). *Teaching language in context*. Heinle & Heinle.

Hedrick, W. B., Harmom, J. M., & Linerode, P. M. (2004). Teachers' beliefs and practices of vocabulary instruction with social studies textbooks in Grades 4-8. *Reading Horizons, 45*(2), 103-125.

Hill, M., & Laufer, B. (2003). Type of task, time-on-task and electronic dictionaries in incidental vocabulary acquisition. *IRAL, 41*, 87-106. https://doi.org/10.1515/iral.2003.007

Huckin, T., & Coady, J. (1999). Incidental vocabulary acquisition in a second language. *Studies in Second Language Acquisition, 21*(2), 181-193. https://doi.org/10.1017/S0272263199002028

Hulstijn, J. H. (2003). Incidental and intentional learning. In C. J. Doughty & M. H. Long (Eds), *The handbook of second language acquisition* (pp. 349-381). Blackwell. https://doi.org/10.1002/9780470756492.ch12

Ito, K. (2015). *Recast and elicitation: the effectiveness of corrective feedback on Japanese language learners*. Master's thesis. University of Massachusetts. https://scholarworks.umass.edu/cgi/viewcontent.cgi?article=1209&context=masters_theses_2

Jackson, J. (2014). *Introducing language and intercultural communication*. Routledge. https://doi.org/10.4324/9781315848938

Klapper, J. (2008). Deliberate and incidental: vocabulary learning strategies in independent second language learning. In T. Lewis & S. Hurd (Eds), *Language learning strategies in independent settings* (pp. 159-178). Multilingual Matters. https://doi.org/10.21832/9781847690999-011

Krashen, S. (1989). We acquire vocabulary and spelling by reading: additional evidence for the input hypothesis. *Modern Language Journal, 73*(4), 440-463. https://doi.org/10.1111/j.1540-4781.1989.tb05325.x

Kruidenier, J. (2002). *Research-based principles for adult basic education reading instruction*. National Institute for Literacy & the Partnership for Reading. https://doi.org/10.1037/e561252012-001

Laufer, B., & Nation, P. (2013). Vocabulary. In S. M. Gass & A. Mackey (Eds), *The Routledge handbook of second language acquisition* (pp. 163-176). Routledge.

Lems, K., Miller, D. L., & Soro, M. T. (2010). *Teaching reading to English language learners: insights from linguistics*. The Guilford Press.

Leow, R. (2015). *Explicit learning in the L2 classroom: a student-centered approach*. Routledge.

Lightbown, P. M., & Spada, N. (2013). *How languages are learned*. Oxford University Press.

Lutz, S., & Huitt, W. (2003). Information processing and memory: theory and applications. *Educational Psychology Interactive*. Valdosta State University.

Nagy, W., Herman, P., & Anderson, R. (1985). Learning words from context. *Reading Research Quarterly, 20*(2), 233-253. https://doi.org/10.2307/747758

Nation, I. S. P. (1999). *Teaching and learning vocabulary*. Heinle & Heinle.

Nation, I. S. P. (2001). *Learning vocabulary in another language.* Cambridge University Press. https://doi.org/10.1017/CBO9781139524759

Nation, I. S. P. (2003). Materials for teaching vocabulary. In B. Tomlinson (Ed.), *Developing materials for language teaching* (pp. 394-405). Continuum.

Ornstein, P. A. (1992). Children's memory for salient events: implications for testimony. In M. L. Howe, C. J. Brainerd & V. F. Reyna (Eds), *Development of long-term retention* (pp. 135-158). Springer-Verlag. https://doi.org/10.1007/978-1-4612-2868-4_4

Read, J. (2001). *Assessing vocabulary.* Cambridge University Press.

Sankey, H. (1991). Incommensurability, translation and understanding. *The Philosophical Quarterly, 41*(165), 414-426. https://doi.org/10.2307/2220077

Schmitt, N. (2010). *Vocabulary in language teaching.* Cambridge University Press.

Shahpari, N., & Shamshiri, H. R. (2014). Intentional vs. incidental vocabulary learning & Iranian EFL learners' retention. *Enjoy Teaching Journal, 2*(3), 1-11.

Sickinger, P. (2017). Aiming for cognitive equivalence – mental models as a tertium comparationis for translation and empirical semantics. *Research in Language, 15*(2), 213-236. https://doi.org/10.1515/rela-2017-0013

Sofer, M. (2005). *Translator self-training: a practical course in technical translation.* Schreiber Publishing.

Stevenson, A. (Ed.). (2010). *Oxford English dictionary* (3rd ed.). Oxford University Press.

Stone, B., & Urquhart, V. (2008). *Remove limits to learning with systematic vocabulary instruction.* Mid-continent Research for Education.

Tabrizi, A. R. T., & Feiz, F. S. (2016). The effect of deliberate versus incidental vocabulary learning strategy on Iranian high school students' vocabulary learning. *World Wide Journal of Multidisciplinary Research and Development, 2*(3), 1-8.

Taylor, L. (1990). *Teaching and learning EFL Vocabulary.* Prentice Hall.

Thelen, M., & Lewandowska-Tomaszczyk, B. (2010). *Meaning in translation (Łódź studies in language).* Peter Lang Publishing Group.

Ur, P. (2012). *A course in English language teaching.* Cambridge University Press.

Whyatt, B. (2009). Building L2 communicative confidence through interlingual tasks: towards function-focused L2 learning. In M. Dynel (Ed.), *Advances in discourse approaches* (pp. 365-388). Cambridge Scholars Publishing.

Wilkins, D. A. (1972). *Linguistics in language teaching.* MIT Press.

Wilkins, D. A. (1974). *Second-language learning and teaching.* Edward Arnold.

Chapter 3

Zandieh, Z., & Jafarigohar, M. (2012). The effects of hypertext gloss on comprehension and vocabulary retention under incidental and intentional learning conditions. *English Learning Teaching, 5*(6), 60-71. https://doi.org/10.5539/elt.v5n6p60

Zojer, H. (2009). The methodological potential of translation in in second language acquisition: re-evaluating translation as a teaching tool. In A. Witte, T. Harden & A. R. O. Harden (Eds), *Translation in second language learning and teaching* (pp. 31-52). Peter Lang.

4 Translation training and language instruction at the academic level

Małgorzata Kodura[1]

Abstract

The aim of this paper is to make a point in a discussion whether and to what extent it is advisable to incorporate language instruction activities into the translation course. Although translation competence is often perceived as a set of sub-competencies that always includes language skills, regardless of the theoretical framework adopted, it is generally assumed that language proficiency of students taking a translation course at the university is adequate to undertake such tasks. However, as experience shows, novice translators frequently struggle with language problems unexpected at that level. Based on an experiment conducted with students of English philology attending a translation course at the Pedagogical University of Cracow, the author of this paper presents challenges and areas of linguistic problems faced by inexperienced translators, proposing solutions that might be useful for a translation trainer designing such a course. A reference is made to a reversed concept of translation as the fifth skill in learning a foreign language. This controversial idea of using translation in a language class, rejected by the modern language teaching approach as deriving from the traditional grammar-translation method, has been recently gaining popularity among teachers and researchers. The findings in this area may be of practical value for both translation teachers and language instructors.

Keywords: translator training, language instruction, L2 teaching methods, translation.

1. Pedagogical University of Cracow, Cracow, Poland; malgorzata@kodura.pl

How to cite this chapter: Kodura, M. (2019). Translation training and language instruction at the academic level. In B. Loranc-Paszylk (Ed.), *Rethinking directions in language learning and teaching at university level* (pp. 75-94). Research-publishing.net. https://doi.org/10.14705/rpnet.2019.31.892

Chapter 4

1. Introduction

The relation between language teaching and translation has always been very close, though turbulent, and of a 'love-hate' type. Those two ideas have been even referred to as 'strange bedfellows' (Carreres, 2006). Throughout history, this relation was typically described in terms of the tool and the aim, often taking extreme points of view, which will be presented in the first part of this paper. Although in discussions concerning those two concepts the focus is typically on applying translation methods in foreign language teaching, this paper will assume an entirely different perspective, namely the issue of language instruction in a translation class, based on the author's experience in teaching undergraduate students in the English department of the Pedagogical University of Cracow.

2. A brief history of the relations between translation and language learning

2.1. Translation as the only L2 teaching method

Translation is considered to be the oldest method of teaching foreign languages, which was widely used for centuries as a classical, unquestionable method of teaching Greek and Latin (Marqués Aguado & Solís-Becerra, 2013, p. 38; Munday, 2001, p. 8). The same approach was later transferred into the way of teaching modern languages, the so-called 'grammar translation' method, introduced in secondary schools in Prussia at the end of the eighteenth century to teach numerous groups of students demonstrating different levels in learning abilities (Anderman, 2007, p. 52; Ferreira, 1999, p. 356). The method consisted in studying the grammar of a language and reading texts, typically of religious or literary natures, with the use of a dictionary and the acquired grammar (Malmkjær, 1998, p. 2).

The first grammar-translation course in English was published in 1793 by Johann Christian Fick, following the model of a course in French proposed by

Johann Valentin Meidinger (Curtis, 2017, p. 148; Pym & Ayvazyan, 2016, p. 3; Randaccio, 2012, p. 78). This method used translation, to and from the foreign language, of individual sentences which were usually specifically constructed to exemplify certain grammatical features. The method was centred on learning the grammatical rules and structures of the foreign language by heart, and on practising and testing the rules and structures acquired through the translation of a series of artificially constructed and separate sentences exemplifying the items studied (Munday, 2001, p. 8). The difficulty of examples was typically graded, which made it possible to teach grammar in a systematic manner. The units of the course were based on grammatical constructions, ordered according to the difficulty levels, and presented in the sentences to be translated and studied (Ferreira, 1999, p. 356). This method was popularised in England in the second half of the eighteenth century with the introduction of the Cambridge Assessment system in 1848, offered by the University of Cambridge Local Examinations Syndicate (UCLES). The idea behind using a grammar-translation method was based on the need to place modern languages on the curriculum along with classical languages. As Randaccio (2012, p. 78) explains, to enjoy the same academic reputablity as the classical languages, modern languages had to be taught using the same teaching methods.

2.2. Translation excluded from the L2 classroom

However, the approach towards the grammar translation method and the use of L1 in the classroom was brought into question and consequently condemned along with the development of new language teaching methods known as the natural method, the conversation method, the direct method, and the communicative approach. The changes were introduced along with the reform movement of the nineteenth century based on new assumptions of language learning which included the primacy of speech, the importance of connected texts in teaching and learning and the priority of oral classroom methodology (Ferreira, 1999, p. 356; Laviosa, 2014, p. 8; Randaccio, 2012, p. 78). The reformers postulated that the exercises consisting in translation into the foreign language should be replaced by practising free composition written in the second language related to subjects already known from previous classes (Sweet, 1900,

p. 206 in Laviosa, 2014, p. 8). Translation into the native language was excluded from the classroom, especially in prestigious language courses boasting the fact of applying modern teaching methodology. For instance, in Berlitz's schools, where the natural method was applied on a large scale, translation was ruled out under any circumstances, which was clearly specified in the directions included in all the teaching books, warning the teacher against even minor concessions on this point (Randaccio, 2012, p. 79).

In this new reality of teaching languages, with the communicative approach coming to the fore, based on the idea that learning language successfully comes through having to communicate real meaning, translation exercises were treated as the factor inhibiting language acquisition. Some of the objections raised against the use of translation in the classroom, organised and formulated by Newson (1998, pp. 63-64), were based on the assumptions that translation encourages thinking in one language, which inevitably causes interference and may support a false belief that word-to-word equivalence between languages exists. Newson (1998) emphasised that translation in the classroom does not facilitate achievement of main language teaching aims such as focus on fluency, attention to gradual introduction of controlled and selected lexical items, or communicative language use, and deprives the teacher of the possibility of observing learning effects in the form of, for example, new ranges of vocabulary or structures. As mentioned by Svěrák (2013),

> "[t]he latter is not surprising since each translation task provides normally only one (random) example of new language items; there is no repetition and practice as in classic forms of language learning and teaching, no grading and no structuring" (p. 54).

2.3. Translation turn in L2 learning

The relation between translation and language began to improve in the mid 1980's, which was both related to a growth of translation studies as an autonomous discipline and to the observations made by experts in methodology and linguistics based on actual use of L1 in the classroom, its advantages, and disadvantages. A renewed interest in translation as part of language classroom practice, begun by Duff (1994), was based on a shift from the emphasis from learning translation as an aim in itself to using translation as a means to promote language learning (Laviosa, 2014, p. 26). Duff, a lecturer and a translator himself, formulated clear arguments for using translation in the classroom, as it develops the ability to "search for the most appropriate words in order to convey accurately the meaning of the original text, thus enhancing flexibility, accuracy and clarity" (Laviosa, 2014, p. 26).

Another author contributing to the reconsideration of translation in language teaching, Cook (2010), presented in his book *Translation in Language Teaching*, a view of the translation as an aid not only to language acquisition, pedagogy, and testing, but also a response to student needs, rights, and the tool of empowerment. As Cook (2010) claims, "I shall argue that for most contemporary language learners, translation should be a major aim and means of language learning, and a major measure of success" (p. xv).

This bold statement acted as a spur for modern scholars to address arguments against translation in language teaching methodology and to provide scientific evidence to legitimate its use in the language classroom, from which, despite the prescription of the communicative approach methodology, it has never been entirely eradicated (Carreres, 2014; Gross, 2013; Kelly & Bruen, 2016; Kupske, 2015; Marqués Aguado & Solís-Becerra, 2013; Pym & Ayvazyan, 2016). Also, books have started to emerge with practical examples of translation activities in foreign language teaching, such as *Translation and Own-language Activities* by Kerr (2014), encouraging the use of translation in a methodologically justified manner, following the assumption translation is a mental process naturally occurring in the heads of our students and trying to exploit this fact for methodological purposes.

In the opinion of researchers following this trend (Duff, 1994, p. 7; Kerr, 2014, p. 122; Pym et al., 2013, p. 135; Randaccio, 2012, p. 81; Schäffner, 1998, p. 125), arguments put forward in favour of using translation in L2 teaching and learning can be summarised as follows:

- it encourages conscious learning, helping to control the foreign language and to reduce negative transfer, improving the understanding of differences between languages;

- it helps young learners (teenagers) at the initial stage of learning of new vocabulary and provides an effective approach in solving the problem of false friends;

- translation makes the learning process meaningful, with the learner involved as an active participant in the process;

- it is an activity that might stimulate the cognitive potential of learners;

- it helps to improve verbal performance by reverbalisation and reformulation of the source text;

- translation activities make learners use the structures that otherwise would be avoided by them;

- it helps to address cultural linguistic differences and promotes correct use of idioms;

- it helps in monitoring and improving the comprehension of the foreign language, thus leaving more time and space for actual language practice; and

- it is associated with high involvement and satisfaction of students.

The argument for the use of translation in the language classroom can be also found directly in the Common European Framework of Reference (CEFR) for languages, a document providing a comprehensive basis for the elaboration of language syllabuses and curriculums, guidelines for preparing teaching and learning materials, and for measuring foreign language proficiency, covering the cultural context in which language is used (Council of Europe, 2001, p. 1). The document clearly mentions the skill of mediation, understood as interpreting and translating, providing the specific examples of mediating activities to be used, such as simultaneous interpretation in meetings or formal speeches, consecutive interpretation, e.g. in guided tours or interpretation in social and transactional situations, translation of contracts and scientific texts, or summarising gist, also between L1 and L2 (Council of Europe, 2001, p. 87).

Therefore, since it is explicitly recommended for teachers to introduce such activities in the foreign language classroom, they should not feel 'guilty' of using and encouraging the use of the mother tongue to practise such skills.

3. The concept of pedagogical translation

What must be clearly emphasised in the translation revival approach is its use as a didactic means and not as the ultimate aim of the classroom activities. This is reflected in the notion of pedagogical translation, a term typically defined in opposition to the so-called 'real translation', with the two concepts differing in the aspect of function, object and addressee. In pedagogical translation, the function of the translated text is to act as a tool for improving language proficiency, consciousness-raising, practising, or testing language knowledge, but also for illumination and memorisation, while in real translation, the translated text is not a tool, but the very goal of the process (Klaudy, 2003, p. 133; Vermes, 2010, p. 83). As regards the object, in pedagogical translation it is information about the language learners' level of language proficiency, while in real translation, it is information about reality contained in the source text. As for the addressee, in translation for pedagogical purposes, the addressee is the language teacher or the examiner, while in real translation it is the target language reader wanting some information about reality.

In the light of this definition, the question emerges whether translation pedagogy, i.e. translation training, is more like pedagogical translation, therefore somehow entitled to follow the same methodology, or is it teaching 'real translation'. Interesting conclusions can be drawn when analysing the notion of translation pedagogy using the same framework. Although in translation training classes, the translated text is the final product of students' work, the function of class translation is also to improve their translation competence, which involves language proficiency and language awareness raising. The object of a translation task is to obtain information about the students' proficiency in writing texts in L1 or L2, with an additional factor of translation accuracy. And the addressee is obviously the teacher – in this case often referred to as the 'translation trainer'. Even on those rare occasions when the product of students' work is indented to be used by general public (e.g. translation of university websites), it is always the teacher or peer students who proofread and evaluate the translation.

It is also worth mentioning that the concept of pedagogical translation vs. real translation corresponds to another dichotomy proposed by Gile (1995) between school translation and professional translation, where school translation is understood as drafting texts based on lexical and syntactic choices prompted by the source-language text, serving "mostly as drills for the acquisition of foreign-language vocabulary and grammar structures and as foreign-language proficiency tests" (p. 26), i.e. serving the students themselves, while professional translation focusses on the reader interested in the contents of the source message, with the purpose of helping people communicate in specific situations. It also reflects the distinction between translation exercises in language teaching and the teaching of translation for a professional career, as introduced by Schäffner (1998, pp. 131-132). In her opinion, the concept of translation in those two situations must be defined in a different way, with translation for foreign language learning aiming being a kind of decoding-encoding translation, i.e. aiming at "reproducing the message of the ST while paying attention to different linguistic structures", and translation training for professional purposes oriented towards "text production for specific purposes" (Schäffner, 1998, pp. 131-132).

4.   Classification of translation students' errors

Therefore, what is the place of language learning in translation teaching? A partial answer to this question was provided by Pym (1992, pp. 4-5), who proposed an interesting division of errors made by students into binary and non-binary ones. Binary errors are those that elicit the teacher's answer 'it is wrong' (in terms of grammar, spelling, or language rules) and that should be subject to a very quick correction. Non-binary errors, on the other hand, require further discussion, explanation, and elaboration. These are the items provoking the answer 'it does not sound good', which, obviously, need a further analysis, thus leading to acquisition of translation competence, understood as the union of two skills:

- the ability to generate a Target Text (TT) series of more than one viable term (TT1, TT2...TTn) for a Source Text (ST); and

- the ability to select only one TT from this series, quickly and with justified confidence, and to propose this TT as a replacement of the ST for a specified purpose and reader (Pym, 1992, p. 3).

It is commonly believed that the 'binary' type errors are to be dealt with in language classes, while the 'non-binary' errors belong to translation training.

To illustrate the issue, some examples of students' errors are provided below. The sentences come from a class translation exercise, consisting in translation of the minutes of the shareholders' meeting into English, as a part of a specialised translation course in the second year of undergraduate studies, discussed in more details in Kodura (2017).

- Dnia dwudziestego ósmego marca dwa tysiące szesnastego roku.
  = *Twenty eight of march in the year two thousand and sixteen*

- Nikt z obecnych nie wniósł sprzeciwu.
  = *None of the present persons has not raised any objections.*

- Obrady Zwyczajnego Zgromadzenia Wspólników otworzył Pan Adam Nowak, który został wybrany na Przewodniczącego.
  = *The session of the Ordinary Shareholders' Meeting opened Mr Adam Nowak, which was voted for the chairman.*

Chapter 4

- Obrady Zwyczajnego Zgromadzenia Wspólników.
  = *Sessions of the General Assembly of Partners*

As it can be easily seen, most of the above errors have been generated by interference from Polish, as we can observe here problems with spelling (the different use of capital letters in both languages), double negation transferred from Polish, incorrect word order). The second year students of English philology are not expected to make such mistakes, and actually, they are very careful with language and do not commit such mistakes in other language classes, yet in the process of translation they become so engrossed in the translation activity itself, i.e. the process of rendering the message in the target language, that they forget to reflect on grammar correctness and possible negative transfer. In the examples quoted above, both binary and non-binary errors can be observed. The first three examples refer to the language, i.e. can be classified as binary errors, while the fourth translation depends on the context and the proper rendering of the source phrase requires proper decoding of the original message supplemented with specific background subject-matter knowledge concerning different types of commercial companies in Poland.

5. Translation activities in the L2 teaching methodology

The examination of students' errors in class and homework assignments led to the conclusion that translation students indeed need some additional language practice in the sense of traditional development of integrated skills, yet with the focus on possible translation issues and especially negative transfer from the mother tongue. The framework for such an approach could be found in ready-made solutions proposed by language experts supporting the idea of using translation activities in the L2 class. Such a framework, with actual examples of class activities, has been proposed, among others, by Leonardi (2010), who grouped them into pre-translation, translation, and post-translation tasks. Examples of the pre-translation activities involve brainstorming, vocabulary preview, or anticipation guides. The activities carried out during the translation activity itself may involve reading activities, summary translation, re-translation or 'back-translation', vocabulary building or even improvement of intercultural awareness, which is the aspect currently emphasised in language teaching curricula. Post-translation activities may include writing a summary of the source text or a translation commentary, which is a valuable element in a translator's training (Leonardi, 2010, p. 88).

Therefore, if the framework for translation activities in language learning is already provided and justified, why not use it in translation class to improve language proficiency?

There are several objections to the concept of combining language instruction and translation training. First of them being the claim popular among translation trainers that translation class is not a good place to develop language skills as students already have blocks of integrated skills courses to deal with such problems, while only 30 hours is intended for translation course, so students should spend them for more 'translation-oriented' activities. Secondly, as Klaudy (2003) claims, "translator training starts where foreign language teaching ends" (p. 133), the assumption being that translator training should start after target language acquisition and the translation trainees are already at an appropriate language level to translate. As it could be observed in the analysis of translation students' errors, it is not always the case. Another opinion supports the claim that translation competence is psychologically complex and differs from language skills, and consequently, should be trained separately (Lado, 1964, p. 54 in Marqués Aguado & Solís-Becerra, 2013, p. 39). The last point to be made here is that the very idea to teach translation into a non-mother tongue is strongly criticised and such a practice is considered artificial. It is claimed that translation into the non-native language induces learners to make errors (Randaccio, 2012, p. 82). Translating into a foreign language is often disapproved by translation experts and professional translators, who claim that regardless of the translator's knowledge of a foreign language, the non-native speaker is not able to produce a text matching that of the competent native speaker (Ross, 2014, p. 5). The non-native speaker is more likely to produce a target text that sounds unnatural or to make language mistakes which may lead to problems with proper interpretation of the source text. Nevertheless, in their future professional work, translation trainees will be expected to translate into their L2, as this is the current translation market situation in Poland, therefore, in spite of strong arguments against practising translation into L2, such activities must be a part of the translator training course, which justifies the need of improving English language competence in translation classes.

6. The study

In order to prove whether development of English language skills is advisable in translation classes, a small-scale study was conducted involving translation students of the Pedagogical University of Cracow. The aim of the study was to answer the question whether introduction of typical language practice exercises is beneficial for students or imposes additional burdens, and to verify the impact of this additional practice on development of overall translation competence. The research tool applied was a comparative analysis of translation performance of two groups of students exposed to alternative translation training methods. Participants were second year undergraduate students attending a course in specialised translation. The study consisted in applying two different teaching methods while carrying out the same block of translation activities related to business texts. The groups were made of 15 and 14 participants, respectively. The block covered five lesson units and corresponded to ten class hours, conducted in a different way for each of the group. Apart from class work, which consisted of translation of the same text for both groups, one of the groups was given an additional short translation task directly related to the class work, while the other group was involved into a typical language development activity using the same text as a base. For example, when the main text to be translated by students was a fragment from a website of a Polish Information Technology (IT) company, the first group was given an additional translation of an English text related to a similar IT company, while the other was exposed to the same text, yet not with the purpose of translating, but filling in the missing words, i.e. completing a reading comprehension type task. Other activities involved finding and using phrasal verbs and collocations in sentences created by students. Tasks given to students included grammar practice exercises, e.g. providing a correct form of verbs to be used in the text (based on the original text prepared by the teacher) or filling in the missing articles or prepositions. Additionally, the group was asked to spot and correct errors in translated texts – errors of the 'binary' type, following classification by Pym (1992). After completing a course unit, the students were given a translation assignment from Polish to English, the same for both groups. Students were asked to translate a 200-word text taken from a website of a Polish IT company (netventure.pl), which closely corresponded to the type of translation and language activities covered during the course (the full source text for the final assignment is provided in the supplementary materials[2]). The aim of this test was to verify whether the mode of conducting the translation course and additional grammar and vocabulary exercises introduced affected, in any way, students' overall translation competence. The task was completed in a class setting, with a time limit of 90 minutes. Both groups took the test on the same day. Students worked independently, without the assistance on the part of the teacher, but could use any Internet-based sources and their own notes. Translated texts were saved in the Word format and uploaded on the Moodle platform. Students' translations were assessed using a scale of 0–20 points, with the maximum score of 20 points, where ten points could be obtained for accuracy and ten for language quality.

7. Study results

After grading translations provided by students of both groups, it was found out that the differences were not very significant, as the average score for group A, who followed the course with additional language exercises, was 16.13, and for group B, 14.79. A difference in the score obtained for the language use in both groups was slightly bigger (7.60 vs. 6.64) than for the translation accuracy (8.53 vs. 8.14). The lowest score obtained in group A was 12 and the highest was 20, while in group B it was 12 and 19, respectively, so individual differences between members of the groups were not that substantial (Figure 1).

---

2. https://research-publishing.box.com/s/5hd0zta9zg83kuj1isj0a8kw6jz0mfzz

Chapter 4

Figure 1. Results of the translation assignment

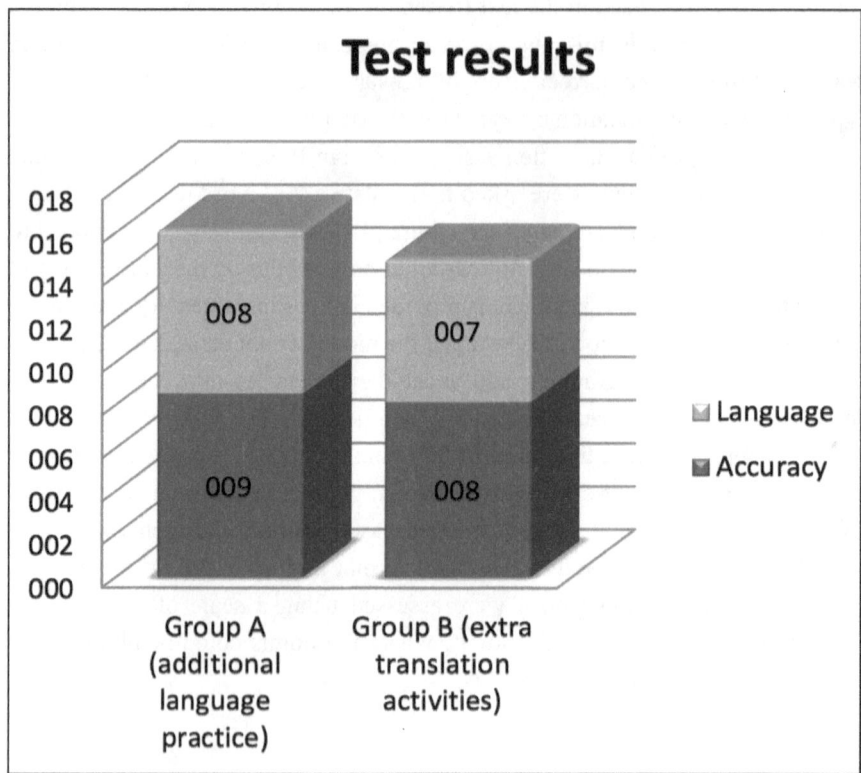

However, the differences are particularly visible in the score obtained for the language use, where the group with additional language practice obtained on average 7.60 points, and the group with extra translation activities only 6.64 points. As regards errors committed by translation trainers, their range was quite varied in both groups under consideration and very frequently they belonged to the binary-type group. This example concerns tenses in English,

- In 2010 newly created Netventure Sp. z o.o. has taken charge of service provision.

- We supported firms in e-marketing when the Internet developed.

this one grammar structures and spelling issues,

- The dynamic development of our services have benefited by implementing neccesary shift.

- People with not only specialistic knowledge but also personal involvment in constant development of the firm create Netventure.

as well as having examples of calques from the Polish language,

- (…) www website

- (…) freshly developing Internet Network

- As an interactive agency, we executed website projects (…)

Errors of this type were observed in both groups, with a slightly better language quality found for the group with additional language practice (7.60 vs. 6.64). However, even the small sample of examples presented above shows that the translation trainer faces a special challenge to focus both on development of language accuracy and on translation competence of students.

At this point, certain limitations of this study must be mentioned. First of all, the groups of students who participated in this test were relatively small, and their overall or language score might be the result of their overall language skills, which in such small groups could significantly affect the final results. Secondly, the time devoted to the study (ten class hours) was too short to radically affect the level of students' competence, although the overall aim of the activities was rather to make students aware of potential vocabulary and grammar problems. Finally, assessing students' work by deducting points for specific language errors is always believed to include an element of subjectivity. Although the grading scale applied in this study was based on many years of teaching practice, the results would be even more reliable if the translated texts were checked by two independent trainers. Nevertheless, the main objective of the study was achieved, i.e. the question whether introduction of extra language exercises is a benefit or a burden for translation students was found, as it turned out that such a form of non-standard translation training was not detrimental to students' acquisition of translation competence, and actually they scored better when exposed to various types of class practice.

There are also some general conclusions that can be derived from the study, and which might be of significant importance to any teacher designing a translation course. Quite interestingly, language activities were well received by students, which might be caused by the fact that they are more used to language development exercises than to translation tasks. It could be also observed that students got more involved in class activities, for instance by taking more notes while doing language exercises, writing down certain collocations or idioms. In their translation assignments, students used the elements they learned through language activities (for example the phrase 'end-to-end solutions'), which is a desirable effect of language practice classes. Students' involvement resulted from an increased attractiveness of the class practice structure, since it was varied and included elements of diversified length (e.g. warm-up activities), as opposed to quite long 'pure' translation tasks, which increased students' motivation to work. By increasing students' motivation based on concepts that are familiar to them (e.g. vocabulary practice), it is easier to encourage them to individually work on the development of their translation competence, which should not be perceived as a set of unrelated sub-competencies, but rather as a post-modern emergent model of translator expertise, or "a holistic bundle" (Kiraly, 2013, p. 201), with a focus on overall development of a novice translator.

However, it should be also added that preparation of class activities is time consuming, since few ready-made exercises are available to match the required context. Language exercises used in translator training must be carefully selected and should particularly focus on differences between languages, e.g. false friends, grammar untranslatability issues, and collocations. However, as the results of this study show, it is certainly worth the effort of the translator trainer. On the other hand, this opens a new demand for L2 learning textbooks based on the latest approach to pedagogical translation, which have gradually started to appear in the educational market (e.g. Carreres, Noriega-Sánchez, & Calduch, 2017). Experienced translator trainers and foreign language teachers could collaborate in the projects targeted at preparing appropriate teaching materials to the benefit of both language students and translation trainees.

8. Conclusions

The introduction of language practice to the undergraduate translation course improves the motivation of students and helps to comprehensively develop their translator competence. In the context of the overall aim of a course focussed on translation skills, properly selected language activities increase the awareness of translation trainees of the existing problems and difficulties resulting from dissimilarities between languages. Equipped with the knowledge acquired in their obligatory courses of contrastive grammar, skills developed during the practical English classes, and additional awareness built during the language activities in translation classes, the students have the opportunity to become better translators and language specialists. The teacher conducting those classes must bear in mind that although undergraduate students at this stage of their tertiary education do not necessarily plan their future as professional translators, they should be provided with the foundations to build their general language competence, as it is recommended, among others, in the CEFR concerning the skills of mediation.

References

Anderman, G. (2007). Linguistics and translation. In P. Kuhiwczak & K. Littau (Eds), *A companion to translation studies* (pp. 45-62). Multilingual Matters Ltd.

Carreres, A. (2006). *Strange bedfellows: translation and language teaching. The teaching of translation into L2 in modern languages degrees: uses and limitations*. 6th Symposium on Translation, Terminology and Interpretation in Cuba and Canada - December 2006. http://www.cttic.org/publications_06Symposium.asp

Carreres, A. (2014). Translation as a means and as an end: reassessing the divide. *The Interpreter and Translator Trainer, 8*(1), 123-135. https://doi.org/10.1080/175039 9X.2014.908561

Carreres, A., Noriega-Sánchez, M., & Calduch C. (2017). *Mundos en palabras: learning advanced Spanish through translation*. Routledge.

Cook, G. (2010). *Translation in language teaching: an argument for reassessment*. Oxford University Press.

Council of Europe. (2001). *Common European framework of reference for languages: learning, teaching, assessment*. Cambridge University Press.

Curtis, A. (2017). *Methods and methodologies for language teaching*. Palgrave.

Duff, A. (1994). *Translation: resource books for teachers*. Oxford University Press.

Ferreira, S. M. G. (1999). Following the paths of translation in language teaching: from disregard in the past to revival towards the 21st century. *Cadernos de Tradução, IV*, 355-371. http://www.journal.ufsc.br/index.php/traducao/article/viewFile/5541/4999

Gile, D. (1995). *Basic concepts and models for interpreter and translator training*. John Benjamins Publishing Company. https://doi.org/10.1075/btl.8

Gross, A. M. (2013). *Translation as a means of learning and self-learning in studying Arabic as a foreign language*. 1st Eurasian Multidisciplinary Forum EMF 2013, 24-26 October 2013, Tbilisi, Georgia, Proceedings (Vol. 2, pp. 487-502). https://annegretmgross.files. wordpress.com/2016/05/publishedannegret-gross-translation-as-a-means-of-learning-and-self-learning-in-studying-arabic-as-a-foreign-language.pdf

Kelly N., & Bruen, J. (2016). Translation as a pedagogical tool in the foreign language classroom: a qualitative study of attitudes and behaviours. *Language Teaching Research, 19*(2), 150-168.

Kerr, P. (2014). *Translation and own-language activities*. Oxford University Press.

Kiraly, D. (2013). Towards a view of translator competence as an emergent phenomenon: thinking outside the box(es) in translator education. In D. Kiraly, S. Hansen-Schirra & K. Maksymski (Eds), *New prospects and perspectives for educating language mediators* (pp. 197-222). Gunter Narr.

Klaudy, K. (2003). *Languages in translation*. Scholastica.

Kodura, M. (2017). Online terminology resources in teaching translation of specialised texts. In B. Borkowska-Kępska & G. Gwóźdź (Eds), *LSP perspectives 2. Języki specjalistyczne - nowe perspektywy 2* (pp. 63-72). Wydawnictwo Naukowe Wyższej Szkoły Biznesu w Dąbrowie Górniczej.

Kupske, F. F. (2015). Second language pedagogy and translation: the role of learners' own-language and explicit instruction revisited. *Brazilian English Language Teaching Journal, January-June, 6*(1), 51-65.

Lado, R. (1964). *Language teaching: a scientific approach*. McGraw-Hill.

Laviosa, S. (2014). *Translation and language education. Pedagogic approaches explained*. Routledge. https://doi.org/10.4324/9781315764542

Leonardi, V. (2010). *The role of pedagogical translation in second language acquisition. From theory to practice*. Peter Lang. https://doi.org/10.3726/978-3-0351-0071-6

Malmkjær, K. (Ed.). (1998). *Translation and language teaching: language teaching and translation*. St. Jerome Publishing.

Marqués Aguado, T., & Solís-Becerra, J. A. (2013). An overview of translation in language teaching methods: implications for EFL in secondary education in the region of Murcia. *Revista de Lingüística y Lenguas Aplicadas, 8*, 38-48. https://doi.org/10.4995/rlyla.2013.1161

Munday, J. (2001). *Introducing translation studies: theories and applications*. Routledge.

Newson, D. (1998). Translation and foreign language learning. In K. Malmkjær (Ed.), *Translation and language teaching: language teaching and translation* (pp. 63-68). St. Jerome Publishing.

Pym, A. (1992). Translation error analysis and the interface with language teaching. In C. Dollerup & A. Loddegaard (Eds), *The teaching of translation* (pp. 279-288). John Benjamins. https://doi.org/10.1075/z.56.42pym

Pym, A., & Ayvazyan N. (2016). *Linguistics, translation and interpreting in foreign-language teaching context*. http://usuaris.tinet.cat/apym/on-line/translation/2016_transation_teaching_short.pdf

Pym, A., Malmkjær, K., & Gutiérrez-Colón Plana, M. d. M. (2013). *Translation and language learning: the role of translation in the teaching of languages in the European Union. A study*. Publications Office of the European Union. http://www.termcoord.eu/wp-content/uploads/2013/08/European_Commission.pdf

Randaccio, M. (2012). Translation and language teaching: translation as a useful teaching Resource. In F. Gori & C. Taylor (Eds), *Aspetti del la didattica e del l'apprendimento del le lingue*. EUT Edizioni Università di Trieste.

Ross, N. J. (2014). *Translation for communications, language and literature*. EDUCatt.

Schäffner, C. (1998). Qualification for professional translators. Translation in language teaching versus teaching translation. In K. Malmkjær (Ed.), *Translation and language teaching. Language teaching and translation* (pp. 117-133). St. Jerome Publishing.

Svěrák, M. (2013). *Translation in English language teaching.* Master's Diploma Thesis. Masaryk University. https://is.muni.cz/th/398663/ff_m/Martin_Sverak_thesis_final.pdf?

Sweet, H. (1900). *The practical study of languages. A guide for teachers and learners.* Henry Holt and Co.

Vermes, A. (2010). Translation in foreign language teaching: a brief overview of pros and cons. *Eger Journal of English Studies, X,* 83-93.

5 The infinitive in the writing of Czech advanced students of English

Silvie Válková[1] and Jana Kořínková[2]

Abstract

This paper sums up partial results of a long-term project aimed at determining specific needs in teaching advanced English students at the Institute of Foreign Languages of the Faculty of Education, Palacký University, where both authors have been teaching for more than 15 years. In our advanced English students, we have long observed a tendency to make quantitative mistakes, that is to use certain English language structures with a remarkably different frequency than the frequency typical for texts composed by English native speakers. Through a series of quantitative analyses of our students' texts in comparison with authentic English texts, we have been trying to identify the areas of major quantitative discrepancies, which, in turn, helps us make our teaching to advanced students more focussed and effective. The present contribution maps the theoretical background of the functions and usage of various forms of the English infinitive, and comments on the frequency of usage of various forms and syntactic positions of the infinitive in authentic English texts and in texts produced by our 3rd year Bachelor students in the written part of their final English language examination.

Keywords: advanced students of English, infinitive, writing.

---

1. Palacky University of Olomouc, Olomouc, Czech Republic; silvie.valkova@upol.cz

2. Palacky University of Olomouc, Olomouc, Czech Republic; jana.korinkova@upol.cz

How to cite this chapter: Válková, S., & Kořínková, J. (2019). The infinitive in the writing of Czech advanced students of English. In B. Loranc-Paszylk (Ed.), *Rethinking directions in language learning and teaching at university level* (pp. 95-114). Research-publishing.net. https://doi.org/10.14705/rpnet.2019.31.893

Chapter 5

1. Introduction

The present quantitative research into the incidence and usage of the infinitive in texts written by Czech advanced students of English is a part of our long-term project dating from 2013. The project aims at understanding and determining the needs of advanced English learners who study at Palacký University to become English language teachers. Through a series of quantitative analyses, i.e. comparing frequencies of selected linguistic features in native and non-native English texts, we aspire to obtain specific and detailed information about which features to target in our pedagogical intervention in teaching both the theory of English linguistics and practical English language usage.

In our initial analysis, which focussed on syntactic complexity in formal writing (Kořínková & Válková, 2013), we found out that Czech advanced students of English and English native speakers used dependent nominal, relative, and adverbial clauses with similar frequency, and only moderate differences were found in their distribution (i.e. relative clauses were slightly more common in authentic English texts while nominal clauses were slightly more common in the texts written by Czech learners). Greater differences were, however, identified in the incidence of structural varieties of dependent clauses, where Czech students preferred the finite varieties over the non-finite ones. In the case of infinitive clauses, the differences were the most remarkable (i.e. native speakers produced almost twice as many of them in various syntactic positions than our Czech students). Different usage of the infinitive was also reported by other researchers who compared Czech or Slovak speakers (both Slavic languages) of English with native speakers (e.g. Hornová, 2015; Kozáčiková, 2015).

Hornová (2015) analysed a learner corpus of spoken English comprising speech acts by 110 students of the first year of Teaching English as a Foreign Language programmes at three Czech universities whose level of English, according to the Common European Framework of Reference for languages (henceforth CEFR), was determined as B2. She reports that the infinitive, together with the other non-finite verb forms in English, was used by Czech students with lower frequency than by native speakers. She compared the results of her quantitative analysis with corpus data introduced in Biber et al. (1999) and concluded that for the Czech learners, the usage of non-finite verb forms was more appropriate in the nominal syntactic functions whereas their usage in complex noun or adjective phrases proved to be more challenging. The outcomes, according to Hornová (2015), prove that Czech students whose knowledge of English reaches the B2 level have not yet managed the correct usage of the non-finite verb forms, including the infinitive.

Kozáčiková (2015) analysed dependent to-infinitive clauses in selected papers in an international scientific journal *Topics in Linguistics*. Her comparative study shows both similarities and differences in the usage of to-infinitive in articles written by non-native (Slovak) authors and those written by native speakers. Although the author does not explicitly state the level of English of the non-native authors, it can be deduced that due to the fact that they were university teachers and researchers, their level would most probably reach C1 or C2 level, i.e. very close to that of native English speakers. The results of the study show that the number of to-infinitive clauses in native speakers' texts was more than twice higher than in non-native speakers' texts. What was similar was the fact that nominal clauses were the most common and adverbial the least common to-infinitive clauses in both corpora. The author explains the reason for different frequency of the usage of sentence condensation by means of the infinitive in the structural syntactic differences between the two languages.

All the above-mentioned results lead us to our present, more detailed analysis of the incidence of the infinitive as one of the language means that serve the language economy. Moreover, we also resolved to focus on the infinitives following modal verbs or their periphrastic forms in order to find out whether our target group students are also able to formally express the grammatical categories connected with the infinitive (i.e. aspect and voice) or whether their active usage of the infinitive is reduced to its basic form as reported by Hornová (2015), who stated that "[n]o complex form of the infinitive (showing aspect or voice) is used in the whole corpus" (p. 51). For this purpose we decided to analyse a written corpus of Czech advanced English students' texts and also to test the students' ability to use correct simple and also complex forms of the infinitive in a relevant language context (see supplementary material[3]).

2. Literature review

2.1. The infinitive in English and Czech

The infinitive belongs to one of the non-finite verb forms together with the present and past participles and the gerund. The English infinitive can be related to the present or past and it can also express the grammatical categories of aspect and voice. Table 1 offers the overview of various forms of the infinitive as introduced by Dušková (2012, p. 267).

Table 1.   Forms of the English infinitive

infinitive	present	past
active – simple	to write	to have written
active – progressive	to be writing	to have been writing
passive	to be written	to have been written

The active form of the infinitive, as the author states, is more common than the passive. The passive is common in academic prose with *can* or *could* to express possibility, and in combination with *must* or *should*, collective obligation is expressed (Biber, Conrad, & Leech, 2006, p. 183). The present form usually relates the infinitive to the action expressed by the finite verb (e.g. *I am sorry to trouble you*). The past infinitive form expresses the action which happened before the one expressed by the finite verb (e.g. *He is likely to have left*). According to Biber et al. (2006), modal verbs (usually *must* or *should*) combined with the past infinitive express obligation or logical necessity. The combination of modal verbs *may* and *might* with the past infinitive can express a certain degree of doubt about past events or situations. The progressive infinitive stresses the action in progress (e.g. *She seems to be enjoying herself,* or *he appeared to have been*

---

3. https://research-publishing.box.com/s/azc1zca0lnwme4nozgxprnr62mj55zay

continually borrowing money). In conversation (fictional dialogue), progressive infinitives combine with *will* or obligation modals. The modal verb *shall*, which is rather rare, when used, usually occurs with the progressive infinitive.

Various forms of infinitives can be a part of complex verb forms (e.g. after modal verbs) or they can function as a structural variety of the dependent clause types. Due to the fact that "non-finite clauses lack tense markers and modal auxiliaries and frequently lack a subject and subordinating conjunction, they are valuable as a means of syntactic compression" (Greenbaum & Quirk, 1990, p. 286), also known as sentence condensation. As for dependent clause types, the infinitive can condense nominal, relative, as well as adverbial clauses.

There is a wide range of syntactic positions that can be expressed by infinitive clauses. The classification by Biber et al. (2006, p. 259) covers the following (note: the examples of English sentences are from the *Longman Grammar of Spoken and Written English*, either 1999 or 2006 version).

2.1.1. Infinitive as subject

- Subject. *Artificial pearls before real swine were cast by these jet-set preachers.* **To have thought this** *made him more cheerful.*

- Extraposed subject. *It's difficult* **to maintain a friendship**.

According to the corpus findings, subject infinitive clauses (i.e. before the main verb) are relatively rare. In comparison with other registers, they are more common in academic prose. Extraposed infinitive clauses occur in most written registers, they should be regarded as the unmarked choice in comparison with subject clauses (Biber et al., 1999, p. 725). The choice between subject and extraposed subject clauses can be influenced by several factors: register, information structure, grammatical complexity, and personal style. Czech students are familiar with both structures in their mother tongue although the frequency of usage in comparison with English may be different. Czech subject infinitive clauses are rather formal both in the position before the main verb or when extraposed, so their occurrence is not frequent. The following examples of Czech infinitive clauses are taken from the grammar book *Česká mluvnice 2* (Komárek & Petr, 1986, p. 147): *Organizovat je nad jeho síly* or its extraposed version *Je nad jeho síly organizovat*.

It should be also noted here that unlike in English, the condensation by the infinitive of subordinate clauses (not only subject clauses) in Czech is possible almost singularly in situations when the subject of the subordinate clause is the same as the subject of the main clause. Thus we can transform *Pavel se snažil, aby (on sám) přišel včas do školy* into *Pavel se snažil přijít včas do školy*. The sentence *Pavel se snažil, aby děti přišly včas do školy*, however, does not allow for such condensation (Hlavsa, Grepl, & Daneš, 1987, p. 231).

2.1.2. Infinitive as subject predicative

- *My goal now is* **to look to the future**.

Infinitive clauses functioning as subject predicative (in more traditional terminology, e.g. Greenbaum & Quirk, 1990, this position is referred to as subject complement) are relatively common in written registers. They are used to frame a series of points in a discussion (e.g. *The first step in any such calculation is to write the equation for the reaction*), they are often used to specify the nouns *aim, objective, plan, goal, purpose, strategy, task,* or *idea*, and finally they can introduce a method or way of doing something.

In Czech, the structure can be the same with the verb *to be* used in these sentences (e.g. the translation of the sample sentence: *Mým cílem je podívat se na budoucnost*). However, these structures, especially with other copular verbs like *seem* and *appear* would be more frequently used in Czech with finite subordinate clauses (Hornová, 2015, p. 50).

2.1.3. Infinitive as direct object

- *He upset you very much, and I hate* **to see that**.

In the position of direct object both bare and to-infinitive clauses can be used. Bare infinitive clauses are, however, restricted to the usage of a few verbs of perception and modality, thus they are much less common than to-clauses. With to-infinitive clauses, the simple pattern verb + to-clause is the most common (e.g. *I didn't claim to be an authority*), on the other hand the pattern verb + *for* NP + to-clause is rare (e.g. *She waited for the little antelope to protest*). Infinitive clauses are used after reporting verbs (*ask, tell*), verbs of cognitive states (*consider, respect*), perception (*see, hear*), desire (*hope, wish, like*), decision or intention (*decide, plan*), effort (*try, fail*), or modality (*let, help*). Although with different frequency in different registers, the most typical verbs followed by infinitive clauses, according to the corpus findings, are *want, try, seem, begin,* and *like* (Biber et al., 1999, p. 711).

In Czech, the object can be expressed by the infinitive too: e.g. *Viděl svítit hvězdu* (Komárek & Petr, 1986, p. 148). Infinitive objects usually follow verbs expressing mental activities, e.g. *Bratr toužil stát se letcem* (Komárek & Petr, 1986, p. 149), verbs with modal or phase meaning, e.g. *Je nutno celou věc promyslit. Začal psát svou knihu.* (Komárek & Petr, 1986, p. 149).

2.1.4. Infinitive as object predicative

- *Some of these issues dropped out of Marx's later works because he considered them* **to have been satisfactorily dealt with**.

Object predicative, also known as object complement, is used in sentences in which the main verb is complex transitive. Such verbs can be cognition verbs (e.g. *assume, believe, consider, understand*), verbs of intention, desire, or decision (e.g. *choose, expect, like, need, prefer, want, wish*), and verbs of discovery (e.g. *find*). In comparison with transitive or intransitive verbs, complex transitive verbs are less frequent.

Unlike all preceding structures which have similar equivalents in Czech, object predicative expressed by the infinitive is not mentioned in the Czech grammar book so we can expect this structure to be rather avoided by Czech students.

Chapter 5

2.1.5. Infinitive as adverbial

- *A little group of people had gathered by Mrs. Millings* **to watch the police activities on the foreshore.**

In comparison with prepositional phrases and adverbs, which are the most common syntactic realisation of adverbials, non-finite clauses (together with finite clauses, noun phrases, and adverb phrases) are relatively rare. It is necessary to say that different semantic categories of adverbials are not associated equally with the above-mentioned syntactic forms. According to the corpus findings (Biber et al., 1999, p. 787), non-finite clauses (including infinitive clauses) are connected with contingency adverbials (i.e. *cause, reason, purpose, concession, condition,* and *result*).

The usage of the infinitive in Czech adverbial clauses is connected with the meanings of purpose, e.g. *Byl jsem v Praze navštívit sestru* (Komárek & Petr, 1986, p. 150), and comparison, e.g. *Byla to lehčí práce než skládat z lodí pytle.* According to Hornová (2015), "[i]n Czech both finite and non-finite purpose clauses can be used, finite ones prevailing" (p. 51).

2.1.6. Infinitive as noun complement

- *They say that failure* **to take precautions against injuring others** *is negligent.*

Unlike postmodifying clauses, which can occur with almost any head noun, noun complement clauses (or appositive clauses) are connected with a closed set of head nouns and they are rare in conversation. On the other hand, to-infinitive noun complement clauses are particularly common in the news. The head nouns taking to-clauses usually represent human goals, opportunities, or actions (e.g. *chance, attempt, effort, ability, opportunity, decision, plan,* or *bid*).

In Czech, the meaning of apposition can be also expressed by the infinitive, e.g. *Nezbude mi nic jiného než odejít.* Its usage, however, is restricted by the finite verb of the main clauses which must allow for such construction.

2.1.7. Infinitive as noun postmodifier

- *It is a callous thing* **to do**.

The overwhelming majority of relative clauses condensed by the infinitive do not have a subject expressed by a for-phrase. An example of a sentence with the expressed subject can be *That'll be the worst thing for us to do* (Biber et al., 2006, p. 294). There are a few nouns with general meanings which are particularly common in these structures, e.g. *time, thing, way, place(s), stuff, a lot.* The frequency of these nouns depends on the register (Biber et al., 1999, p. 633).

In Czech it is usually nouns expressing some volitional or intellectual activities that are followed by the infinitive (e.g. *přání, úmysl, odvaha, nadání, možnost*) so although this structure is restricted in the usage, Czech speakers are familiar with it.

2.1.8. Infinitive as part of an adjective phrase

- *I think the old man's a bit afraid* **to go into hospital**.

Adjectives followed by infinitive clauses include those which express certainty, willingness, emotion or stance, ease or difficulty, and evaluation. There is one adjective which is very common in Biber et al.'s (2006) corpus, i.e. *(un)likely*, those which are moderately common include *(un)able, determined, difficult, due, easy, free, glad, hard, ready, used,* and *(un)willing* (pp. 335-336).

In Czech, some adjectives can be also followed by the infinitive (e.g. *I'm ready to start. Jsem připraven začít*). The majority, however, would be followed by finite subordinate clauses (*I'm sorry to hear that. Mrzí mě, že to slyším*).

We can conclude this section by stating that Czech students know all the syntactic positions of the infinitive (with the exception of the object predicative) from their mother tongue, although the frequency of their occurrence is not described by the grammar books as identical.

2.2. The CEFR and English Profile

Relating foreign language students' knowledge of various linguistic features to the reference levels described by the Council of Europe (2001) is of high importance for researchers, curriculum designers, teachers, and also language testers. The CEFR levels together with illustrative descriptors can be used for the organisation of both teaching and learning of any language, which makes the CEFR neutral with respect to the language being taught and learnt. Placing the knowledge of specific grammatical features, such as the infinitive, is then rather intuitive as the descriptions are not detailed enough to help us make decisions about the particular level(s) at which its different forms and syntactic functions should be taught and learnt.

According to the CEFR, for the realisation of communicative intentions, learners use their general capacities together with a more specifically language-related communicative competence. This communicative competence comprises linguistic competences, sociolinguistic competences, and pragmatic competences. The grammatical competence, which is one of the linguistic competences, is defined by the Council of Europe (2001) as "the ability to understand and express meaning by producing and recognising well-formed phrases and sentences in accordance with these principles" (p. 113). In terms of grammatical accuracy, at B2 level language users are expected to show a relatively high degree of grammatical control and they do not make mistakes which lead to misunderstanding. At C1 level users consistently maintain a high degree of grammatical accuracy; errors are rare and difficult to spot (Council of Europe, 2001, p. 114). These descriptions, although rather general, can suggest that at B2 and C1 levels learners of English should be able to use the infinitive expressing the grammatical categories of aspect and voice in various syntactic functions. The preceding B1 level associates the grammatical knowledge with routinised patterns and noticeable mother tongue influence, which suggests that simple forms of the infinitive in most syntactic patterns would be associated with this level.

In comparison with the CEFR, *The English Profile Programme* (henceforth EP) is a more specific document available for reference. Its main aim is to describe (but not prescribe) what learners can do with the language at each of the levels described by the CEFR, thus we can also refer to it as the CEFR for English. The EP does not capture all language features that a learner can use at a certain level but focusses on those which distinguish each level from adjacent higher and lower levels (EnglishProfile, 2011, p. 6). This criterial features concept is based on the idea that there are certain linguistic properties characteristic and indicative at each level. The researchers who compiled EP had utilised *The Cambridge Learner Corpus*, which is a large collection of exam scripts written by students who had taken the Cambridge English to Speakers of Other Languages exams around the world. Two types of criterial features were considered in the corpus: correct linguistic properties (i.e. those acquired at a certain level persisting at higher levels), and incorrect properties or errors (occurring at a certain level with a characteristic frequency). Their analysis resulted in the list of key features for each CEFR level. In terms of the infinitive and its usage, simple patterns with the infinitive are typical for A2 a B1 levels, e.g. *I want to buy a coat., ...something to eat, The train station is easy to find* (EnglishProfile, 2011, p. 11). As learners progress through the levels, they acquire more complex structures. At B2 level it is for example a sentence pattern introduced by *It* and followed by an infinitive phrase, e.g. *It would be helpful to work in your group as well* (EnglishProfile, 2011, p. 14), at C1 level other more complex structures with infinitival clauses are acquired, e.g. *The internet is a valuable tool, which can be proved to be the most important aspect in the learning process* (EnglishProfile, 2011, p. 15). The EP is also available online and its internet version gives more details about the respective levels in terms of possible search according to chosen categories, e.g. passives, modality, etc. Thus we learn that it is the level B2 where learners use complex forms of infinitives after modal verbs e.g. *I don't remember how I lost it, it might have been stolen. My composition was ready to be printed and I was searching for a piece of paper.* At this level, as already mentioned above, learners can also use the infinitive in subject or object extraposition, e.g. *It is best to spend your time in the countryside. This shyness makes it hard for me to speak in public, or even to go out with my friends as often as I should* (EnglishProfile, 2015).

Our expectation, based on all above-mentioned information, was that our research group of students at C1 level should have mastered the active usage of infinitive for the purpose of sentence condensation in nominal, relative, and adverbial dependent clauses. At the same time they should be able to produce correct forms of the infinitive (e.g. the past, progressive, or passive infinitive) in complex verb phrases, when stimulated by a relevant grammatical context.

3. Data analysis

3.1. Quantitative analysis of native speakers' and Czech advanced students' English texts

To determine potential quantitative differences in the usage of various forms of the infinitive in the syntactic positions listed in the previous section as identified by Biber et al. (2006), we assembled a corpus of 65 texts, 35 written by Czech advanced learners of English and 30 by native English speakers. The Czech learners were 3rd year students of the Bachelor study programme *English with Focus on Education* at The Faculty of Education, Palacký University, Olomouc. The expected level of their English, as reflected in the design of their curriculum, was C1 according to the CEFR. The students produced the texts in response to the writing task of their final language examination according to the given specifications related to the genre and length of the required output. The time allocated to complete the task was sufficient for them to plan their writing and edit the final result according to their best capacity. The native English corpus included sample texts taken from the writing sections of advanced English course books commonly used for teaching at universities in the Czech Republic and sample texts displayed on the Internet on various web pages focussed on developing advanced writing skills.

All texts in our corpus were formal reports or proposals between 250 and 350 words long. The formal style of writing was selected because it naturally opens the chance to use the infinitive more frequently than in less formal styles. Furthermore, both proposals and reports generally contain a high number of modal verbs, which are always followed by some form of the infinitive. The texts were analysed manually, the occurrence of various structural forms of the infinitive in selected syntactic positions was counted and compared between the Czech Students' texts (henceforth CS) and Native Speakers' texts (henceforth NS). Table 2 introduces the basic data concerning our corpus and the general incidence of the infinitive. As we can observe, the overall occurrence of infinitives was found to be higher in the CS texts, which was rather surprising since it contradicts both our own previous findings as well as the finding by Kozáčiková (2015, see Introduction).

Table 2. General incidence of infinitive in NS and CS texts

	NS	CS
number of texts	30	35
number of words	8,025	8,713
number of infinitives/1,000 words of text	53.5	65.2

3.1.1. Structural forms of the infinitive

As stated above, there are six basic forms of the English infinitive, with the simple infinitive being the most frequent one, and according to the CEFR and the EP, both simple and complex forms of the infinitive should be acquired already at the B2 level. According to the profile of their study programme, our students should have proceeded from B2 on the higher level of C1 some two years ago, and we were therefore interested to find out whether and to what extent this might be reflected in the frequency of other than simple forms of the infinitive in their texts. Table 3 below compares the frequency of occurrence of all six structural forms of the infinitive in the NS and CS texts.

Table 3. Occurrence of simple and complex forms of the infinitive in the NS and CS texts

infinitive	present		past	
	NS	CS	NS	CS
active – simple	85.8%	94.5%	1.8 %	0
active – progressive	0.2%	0	0	0
passive	12%	5.5%	0.2%	0

It is evident that the frequency of the complex forms of the infinitive is remarkably lower in the CS texts. It seems that even at their advanced level of English, our students still heavily rely on the basic easiest form. Out of the six listed forms, they actively produced only two different most commonly used forms of the infinitive (simple active and simple passive), while the native writers used five different forms in total, although the incidence of the complex ones was, with the exception of the passive present infinitive, rare.

3.1.2. Syntactic position of the infinitive

By the syntactic position of the infinitive we mean its placement among the other sentence elements in the given sentence structure. Generally, most infinitives tend to occur as parts of complex verb forms following a modal verb (Biber et al., 2006). In our analysis, this was confirmed in both NS and CS texts, as indicated in Table 4 below. In the CS texts, however, the number of infinitives following a modal verb proved to be only slightly higher than the number of infinitives not following a modal verb. Other syntactic positions, where the infinitive does not follow a modal verb, are listed according to their calculated frequency in the NS texts.

Table 4. Syntactic position of the infinitive in NS and CS texts/1,000 words

infinitive	NS	CS
following a modal verb	31.7	35
other syntactic position	21.8	30.2
– adverbial	6	8.3
– object	5.5	7.7
– noun postmodification	4	2.9
– subject predication	3	6.7
– part of adjective phrase	1.9	0.8
– subject extraposition	1.1	3.7
– object predication	0.3	0
– subject	0	0.1

In both groups of texts, infinitive adverbial and object clauses proved to be the most commonly used ones. This is again in contrast with the conclusions drawn by Kozáčiková (2015), in whose corpus of native and non-native academic texts adverbial infinitive clauses were the least frequent ones. It can be observed that Czech advanced students of English tend to use infinitives more frequently in all listed positions apart from noun and adjective postmodification, and object predication. The reasons for this may vary with respect to the individual syntactic positions and include generally lower repertory of syntactic structures, a possible quantitative transfer from the Czech language, and also direct negative transfer resulting in grammatical mistakes. For example, the high frequency of the adverbial infinitive clauses might be explained by the genres of the texts. Almost all of these clauses fall into the grammatical category of the adverbial clause of purpose, which is a basic common structure to use in a proposal and the recommendation section of a report (and also the only adverbial infinitive clause actively used in Czech (see above). The higher frequency of infinitives used in subject extraposition and subject predication might have been caused by the transfer from the students' mother tongue as both structures are relatively common in formal Czech texts. The negative transfer might also have caused the lower frequency of infinitives in noun and adjective postmodification because these structures are fairly restricted in usage in the Czech language. Another reason for lower incidence of the infinitive in the noun postmodification might be the fact that the Czech language relies more on verbal expression and so the frequency of noun phrases tends to be generally lower. This could be supported by the data obtained in our previous research, where the incidence of noun phrases in texts written by native English speakers was found to be 18 percent higher than in the writing of Czech advanced students of English (Válková & Kořínková, 2015).

Grammatical mistakes seem to be the main cause of the higher frequency of infinitives in the position of the direct object. In fact, if we counted only the grammatically correct infinitives in this syntactic position, their frequency in the CS texts would be even somewhat lower than in the NS texts (4.9/1,000 words of text). This shows that even at an advanced level of English language proficiency some students still have not been able to internalise certain verb patterns typical for English but different in their mother tongue. The most troublesome verbs in this respect proved to be the verbs *suggest, recommend,* and *propose*, which were commonly and incorrectly followed by the infinitive structure in the CS texts (e.g. *I suggest to make new plans, I propose to hire more staff, I recommend to build more parking places*).

3.2. Grammar test

As the quantitative analysis of our students' writing showed that they rarely used the infinitive in other than its simple active form, we decided to find out whether they are actually familiar with the complex forms enough to be able to produce them when guided by a relevant language context.

A short grammar test was devised, based on an adapted version of a fill-in exercise from a course book of practical English morphology by Hardošová (2009). The test comprised ten sentences with 13 blanks to be filled with appropriate forms of the infinitive (see supplementary material[4]). The answer key provided by the course book was consulted with two British English and two American English speakers to clarify the possibility of any alternative answers. The test was administered to 70 students of the 2nd and 3rd year of the Bachelor study programme *English with Focus on Education* at The Faculty of Education, Palacký University, Olomouc. The ability to produce some of the infinitival forms was tested in more than one sentence to see to what extent its formation and usage might be influenced by the syntactic position and general lexical context of the sentence. All answers given for each blank were recorded in the form of a table as illustrated by the example below (Table 5). Although the students were clearly instructed to fill in only relevant forms of the infinitive of the given word, other structures, both grammatically correct and incorrect, were occasionally supplied as well.

Table 5. Answers supplied for Sentence 1 of the grammar test

Sentence 1: You´d better _____ (see) a doctor, you might _____ (break) your finger.					
blank 1	2nd year	3rd year	blank 2	2nd year	3rd year
see	33	23	have broken	26	26
go to see	1	2	broke	4	3
go see	0	1	break	6	2
to see	1	2	have broke	0	2
saw	1	1			
seen	0	3			
seeing	0	1			

---

4. https://research-publishing.box.com/s/azc1zca0lnwme4nozgxprnr62mj55zay

We were rather surprised to find out that there was virtually no difference in the number of correct answers between the two groups of students, which seems to suggest that in this area of English grammar there is little progress between the second and the final third year of students' studies. In some cases, the group of 2nd year students was even slightly more successful than their older colleagues. Overall, the percentage of correct infinitive forms in the former group was 58.8% and in the latter group 59.1%, which does not seem to be a very positive result. The following table lists the percentage of correctly supplied forms of different structural varieties of the infinitive (Table 6). The infinitives are presented in their immediate language context and the index number following each structure indicates the number of the blank in the test (see supplementary material[5]).

Table 6. Percentage of correct answers with respect to structural forms of infinitive

infinitive	present			past		
	structure	2nd year	3rd year	structure	2nd year	3rd year
active – simple	Can't *find*[10]	100%	100%	appears *to have lost*[8]	25%	42%
	vehicle *to meet*[5]	80%	65%	might *have broken*[2]	69%	76%
	make him *turn*[7]	69%	67%	should *have won*[3]	64%	73%
	had better *see*[1]	94%	70%			
active – progressive	seem *to be working*[11]	61%	76%	pretended *to have been painting*[9]	28%	21%
	happen *to be riding*[6]	22%	21%			
passive	expected *to be invited*[4]	78%	82%	must *have been read*[12]	64%	67%
				sorry *to have had to cancel*[13]	11%	9%

It is evident that the ability to use appropriate simple and complex forms of the infinitive does, indeed, depend on more factors than just being able to form the structure itself. Clearly, students were more successful when dealing with a form of infinitive which does have a direct equivalent in their mother tongue and which is presented in a familiar and common lexical context (e.g. compare

---

5. https://research-publishing.box.com/s/azc1zca0lnwme4nozgxprnr62mj55zay

the answers for can't *find*[10] and vehicle *to meet*[5], or expected *to be invited*[4] and sorry *to have had to cancel*[13]. Still, the results clearly support the findings of our quantitative analysis asserting that for our advanced English students, the simple active and present passive forms of the infinitive are the least problematic ones, whereas the progressive forms (both present and past) are the most challenging and avoided ones.

4. Discussion and conclusions

Contrary to our expectations and the results of some previous comparative studies of native and non-native English writing, a noticeably higher incidence of infinitives was observed in the texts produced by the advanced Czech students than in those authored by native English speakers. Some possible reasons for this have been mentioned above and include limited varieties in sentence structure, quantitative transfers from students' mother tongue (preference for structures commonly used in Czech), and qualitative negative transfers leading to grammatical mistakes. The first and the second mentioned reasons might also be reflected in the more common occurrence of modal verbs in the CS texts. It is interesting to note that while their frequency was only slightly higher in the CS reports (24 and 28 modals per 1,000 words of text in the NS and CS writing respectively), it was remarkably higher in proposals (38 vs. 48 modals per 1,000 words of text). This probably suggests that Czech students tend to use less varied structures in the language function of proposing ideas, relying on basic modal verbs, especially *would* and *should*.

A higher proportion of simple infinitives was found, both in students' original writing and in their answers to the administered grammar test. This suggests that even though the students should have reached the advanced level of C1 and should have mastered even the complex and less frequently used grammatical forms, in reality it is not so. Especially the progressive forms of the infinitive did not prove to have been either formally mastered or appropriately used in a relevant linguistic context.

Although this area of English grammar might seem a marginal one, it still contributes to the students' general capacity to effectively express precise ideas when composing English texts, especially formal ones. Since our students are future English teachers, we believe that they should confidently master the system of the English language in as many details as possible. Advanced students of English will benefit both from more focussed exposure to various forms and syntactic positions of infinitives as well as from more extensive practice in their usage. This could entail guided study of authentic English texts, contrasting them with texts written by non-native speakers, practice in reformulation, etc. Activities to help our students broaden and fine-tune their repertory of actively used structures have yet to be designed and tested. We believe that it would be more reasonable and relevant to focus on problematic areas than the usual presentation and practice sequence. The problematic areas should include not only the infinitive but also other linguistic features we have studied so far, i.e. syntactic complexity, coordination and subordination of nominal, relative, and adverbial clauses, non-finite verb forms in subordinate clauses, complex noun phrases, personal pronouns, and the usage of the comma.

There is no agreement among researchers whether the teaching of grammar is worthwhile if the aim is the improvement of the quality and accuracy of written texts. In our experience, at higher levels of language teaching and learning, the linguistic component is less stressed than sociolinguistic and pragmatic components. We believe that more attention paid to the linguistic component and targeted instruction may result in substantial changes in the syntactic and morphological variety of texts written by our students.

References

Biber, D., Conrad, S., & Leech, G. (2006). *Student grammar of spoken and written English*. Longman.

Biber, D., Johansson, S., Leech, G., Conrad, S., & Finegan, E. (1999). *Longman grammar of spoken and written English*. Longman.

Council of Europe. (2001). *Common European framework of reference for languages: learning, teaching, assessment.* Cambridge University Press.

Dušková, L. (2012). *Mluvnice současné angličtiny na pozadí češtiny.* Academia.

EnglishProfile. (2011). *Introducing the CEFR for English.* University of Cambridge.

EnglishProfile. (2015). E*nglish grammar profile.* http://www.englishprofile.org/english-grammar-profile

Greenbaum, S., & Quirk, R. (1990). *A student's grammar of the English language.* Longman.

Hardošová, M. (2009). *Practical English morphology.* Univerzita Mateja Bela, Fakulta humanitních vied.

Hlavsa, Z., Grepl, M., & Daneš, F. (1987). *Mluvnice češtiny 3.* Academia.

Hornová, L. (2015). Syntactic functions of non-finite verb forms in a learner corpus of Czech students. In M. Adam & R. Vogel (Eds), *Communication across genres and discourses. Sixth Brno Conference on Linguistic Studies in English* (pp. 45-58). Masarykova Univerzita.

Komárek, M., & Petr, J. (1986). *Mluvnice češtiny 2.* Academia.

Kořínková, J., & Válková, S. (2013). Syntactic complexity in advanced students' writing. *Journal of Interdisciplinary Philology, 4*(1-2), 45-52..

Kozáčiková, Z. (2015). To-infinitive clauses in academic discourse – native and non-native writers compared. *Discourse and Interaction, 8*(1).

Válková, S., & Kořínková, J. (2015). The complex noun phrase in advanced students' writing. In *From Theory to Practice 2014: Proceedings of the Sixth International Conference on Anglophone Studies.* Zlín: Univerzita Tomáše Bati ve Zlíně.

6 A search for paraphrasing and plagiarism avoidance strategies in the context of writing from sources in a foreign language

Małgorzata Marzec-Stawiarska[1]

Abstract

Writing from sources is a keystone in academic education. Studies show that it can be problematic for students and in extreme cases may result in plagiarism. This article is devoted to one of the many skills necessary to write from sources, namely paraphrasing. The study described here aims to identify and categorise the paraphrasing and plagiarism avoidance strategies applied by students when writing their Master of Arts (MA) dissertations in English as a Foreign Language (EFL). The data were collected via questionnaires and were based on students' reports concerning their paraphrasing behaviours. The study enabled an array of before-, while- and after-paraphrasing strategies to be collected. The results may contribute to the literature on writing from sources by drawing greater attention to strategic behaviours of students connected with paraphrasing and plagiarism avoidance.

Keywords: plagiarism, paraphrasing strategies, intertextual transparency, EFL writing, academic writing.

---

1. Pedagogical University of Cracow, Cracow, Poland; m.marzec.stawiarska@gmail.com

How to cite this chapter: Marzec-Stawiarska, M. (2019). A search for paraphrasing and plagiarism avoidance strategies in the context of writing from sources in a foreign language. In B. Loranc-Paszylk (Ed.), *Rethinking directions in language learning and teaching at university level* (pp. 115-135). Research-publishing.net. https://doi.org/10.14705/rpnet.2019.31.894

Chapter 6

1. Introduction

Connections between reading and writing in an academic writing setting remain largely unexplored (Hirvela, 2004; Plakans, 2009). Their investigation is vital, as tasks combining reading and writing are an important part of academic education. Paraphrasing, together with direct quotation, summarising, and translation, are core skills that students need to develop to be able to write from sources. Although studies on writing from sources in Foreign Language (FL) and L2 contexts have intensified in the last decade, little is known about strategies and behaviours that allow students to paraphrase sources in ways that avoid plagiarism. The aim of the current study is therefore to investigate what strategies students apply while writing their MA dissertations to avoid the potential for plagiarism when paraphrasing texts from FL sources.

2. Defining paraphrasing

Paraphrasing may be defined as "restating a passage from a source in fresh language" (Howard, Serviss, & Rodrigue, 2010, p. 181); however, studies (Hirvela & Du, 2013; Shi, 2012; Yamada, 2003) show that in the context of academic writing commonly known definitions are not enough to signal to students what paraphrasing really embodies. For example, the phrase 'restatement' may be problematic as it suggests that students should report what is in the source text in a different way which, apparently, is not enough (Yamada, 2003). An analysis of paraphrasing in academic writing shows that it goes beyond a mere restating of ideas in other words and frequently requires substantial inferencing and interpreting skills combined with elements of discipline knowledge (Yamada, 2003).

There have been some attempts to identify different types of paraphrasing. Shi (2004) distinguished between 'slightly modified' and 'syntactically reformulated' paraphrases. However, both these types of paraphrases involved modifications of source text of a local character and could be seen as bearing traces of plagiarism. The literature on writing from sources frequently mentions a division of paraphrasing into 'superficial' and 'substantial' (Keck, 2006;

Roig, 1999; Shi, 2012). Superficial paraphrasing encompasses minor text modifications, mainly word substitution, deletion, addition of single words, and rearrangement of a sentence structure (e.g. Keck, 2010; Roig, 1999), whereas substantial paraphrasing involves major modifications of the source text (Keck, 2006). The problem with this division is that it is based on a high degree of subjectivity and fluid boundaries. The most detailed and least subjective division of paraphrase types was proposed by Keck (2006, 2014). She distinguished four paraphrasing types which differ according to the amount of words copied from the original and number of syntactic and lexical transformations performed on the source text: (1) "Near copies [...] contain copied strings of five or more words" and "simplification through synonym substitution and deletion" (Keck, 2014, p. 9); (2) 'Minimal revisions' comprise copied strings of three to four words and numerous substitutions of synonyms; (3) 'Moderate revisions' may copy one to two word phrases and involve substitution of synonyms and change of clause structures; and (4) 'Substantial revisions' involve the borrowing of individual words and revision of clause structures.

2.1. Paraphrasing in a context of writing from sources

Writing from sources necessitates several decisions when a "student locates, and reconstructs, or appropriates material" (Hirvela, 2004, p. 94). It is a complex process because, as Campbell (1990) remarks, it involves "reading, understanding, learning, relating, planning, writing, revising, editing and orchestrating" (p. 211). Apart from understanding the sources, students need to select relevant excerpts in an original text that would serve some particular rhetorical function in their writing. They need to decide on the form of citation, for example whether they want to paraphrase or quote. They need to integrate a cited excerpt in such a way that readers understand the purpose of the citations (e.g. Petrić, 2012). What is more, writers need to make sure that each time readers know "whose voice is speaking" (Groom, 2000, p. 15) and that the boundaries between their own words and the words adapted or copied from sources are clearly marked (e.g. Pecorari, 2003). Students need to acknowledge the sources properly by using a selected citing system, and not only relate the content of the source accurately but also, if needed, relate the author's stance to the presented ideas. In some cases students may also need to indicate their own stance, so-called 'writer stance', to the cited materials (for author and writer stance see Thompson & Ye, 1991), which is connected with building their own authority as writers (Abasi & Akbari, 2008). Relating a writer or author's stance also necessitates appropriate use of reporting verbs (Hyland, 2002; Thompson & Ye, 1991). Furthermore, students need to be familiar with the conventions used within a given discipline and be aware of what constitutes plagiarism in that discipline, as practices of writing from sources and understanding of plagiarism vary across different academic disciplines (Bloch, 2012; Shi, 2012).

Paraphrasing as part of writing from sources has been found to be challenging for students (e.g. Pecorari, 2003, 2008; Shi, 2012) and having to write in their L2 or FL may pose an additional challenge for them. Students, especially novice ones, were observed to extensively rely on copying from sources (Keck, 2006). Students' attempts to paraphrase were found to be based on superficial text modifications which stayed too close to the original text (Howard et al., 2010; Pecorari, 2008; Pecorari & Shaw, 2012; Shi, 2012). This is sometimes referred to as patchwriting, which in turn may qualify as plagiarism (Howard, 1995). The studies show that students' superficial paraphrasing may result from problems with source text comprehension (e.g. Howard et al., 2010). Superficial paraphrasing was also found to be applied by students as a strategy of academic survival (Abasi & Akbari, 2008) – the only resort for students who have to write in their L2 as part of their academic assignments but are new to academic discourse and academic writing. Patchwriting may also be applied as a strategy of learning of how to write academic texts, as by copying the language of sources and rhetorical devices of authors students learn to construct academic texts (e.g. Abasi & Akbari, 2008; Howard, 1995; Pecorari, 2003, 2008). Shi (2012) observed that L2 students had difficulties in understanding how a paraphrase should look and how to paraphrase without plagiarising. Similarly, Roig's (1997) study found that in some instances the students' main criterion for qualifying an excerpt as plagiaristic was whether it contained an author's name and not the extent of text transformation (which resulted in their qualifying paraphrases based on minor modifications as non-plagiaristic). Wette (2010) observed that L2 students had difficulties in selecting citation-worthy text extracts, indicating boundaries between citations and their ideas, incorporating citations in their writing, and developing a "questioning, evaluative stance towards the authority of published texts" (p. 168). Hirvela and Du (2013) found that EFL students had no major problems with paraphrasing when it was performed as an isolated activity but it became problematic for them when writing longer texts. Students' understanding of paraphrasing was found to be rather superficial, and their paraphrases did not reach a rhetorical or conceptual level. They did not perceive themselves as powerful speakers and treated paraphrasing as a "linguistically-oriented rearrangement tool" (Hirvela & Du, 2013, p. 96) rather than a rhetorical device which serves some purpose for their writing. Due to uncertainty about how to paraphrase while writing academic texts they avoided paraphrasing altogether and resorted to direct quotation.

2.2. Paraphrasing as part of tasks combining reading and writing[2]

Paraphrasing combines reading and writing. These processes constantly overlap and interact, as in integrated reading/writing tasks "writing provides a way into reading, extends reading and consolidates understanding of a text just as reading sustains writing and furnishes, for the writer, the counterpart of another voice" (Carson & Leki, 1993, p. 2). In order to paraphrase, students not only need to understand a source text and incorporate it in their writing (a reading-to-write direction), but they also need to approach reading from a writing perspective (a writing-to-read direction). If students have awareness of what they want to achieve through their writing and approach reading with this in mind, they will have a clearer sense of direction and study sources in a way that is selective and relevant to the function and topic of their writing (Hirvela, 2004).

As both reading and writing skills are needed in order to paraphrase, it may be assumed that the strategies applied by students during FL or L2 reading-only tasks

---

[2]. Initially, I had planned to use the term 'reading-to-write' tasks as it is very commonly used in the literature to refer to tasks which combine reading and writing. However, the book by Hirvela (2004) made it very clear that during such tasks students both read-to-write and write-to-read as it is not only reading that influences their writing but also writing that significantly impacts how they analyse and read sources. Hence the term 'reading-to-write' could be slightly misleading in this context as during tasks involving writing from sources there is an intensive bidirectional interplay of reading and writing.

(e.g. Phakiti, 2003) and FL or L2 writing-only tasks (e.g. De Silva, 2010) may to some extent also be applied in integrated reading/writing tasks. Students need to apply a set of FL reading strategies in order to read FL texts effectively, and a set of FL writing strategies to plan, write, and revise their own texts. However, the fact that students need to read-to-write and write-to-read simultaneously makes writing from sources a very specific endeavour which may involve a unique set of strategies typical only for FL reading-writing constructs. Few studies have focussed on this issue: Cohen (1994), Esmaeili (2002), and Plakans (2009) investigated reading strategies applied by students during integrated reading/writing tasks. Plakans's (2009) study resulted in the proposal of a taxonomy of such strategies comprising five major categories: (1) goal-setting, for example checking the task to integrate sources; (2) cognitive processing, for example slowing the reading rate (pausing), breaking lexical items into parts/using phonological cues, rereading passages; (3) global strategies, encompassing for example asking questions, recognising text structure/rhetorical cues; (4) metacognitive, for example recognising lack of comprehension; and (5) mining strategies, for example scanning texts for ideas to use in writing (pp. 257-258). The study also showed that students who achieved higher scores for their essays used more global- and mining-type strategies while the lowest scoring students employed more word-level reading strategies.

As far as writing from sources is concerned, there have also been studies that investigated strategies and behaviours typical for summarising (e.g. Brown & Day, 1983; Johns & Mayes, 1990; Taylor, 1984; Yang & Shi, 2003). For example, very careful reading of the text, spending a considerable amount of time reflecting on the subject of the text and on what to write, thorough analysis of a text's structure, close monitoring of accurate reporting of a source text (Taylor, 1984), constant referring back to the source text, spending extra time on planning and monitoring (Yang & Shi, 2003), and verbalising what is being written (Yang & Shi, 2003) have been identified as strategies or behaviours typical for high quality summaries.

Little is known however about what strategies students use when they paraphrase while writing from sources and what strategies they apply when they try to avoid plagiarism while paraphrasing. Investigating paraphrasing strategies seems worth pursuing as paraphrasing has been found to be challenging for students. Identifying paraphrasing and plagiarism avoidance techniques could help effective instructions in paraphrasing FL source texts to be developed. Providing students with proper instructions on paraphrasing would seem to be a very important aspect of training in academic writing as information available to students on how to write from sources without plagiarising, even those available on highly informative and student-friendly webpages, is definitely inadequate. It was found by Bloch (2012) that students who were thoroughly informed how to write from sources and avoid plagiarism still had problems with putting these rules into practice when writing from sources. Hirvela and Du (2013) observed that "while the procedures involved in paraphrasing source text material may appear simple, the enactment of these procedures is often a complex and elusive experience for L2 writers" (p. 87). Hence this study looks at the strategies students adopt when they paraphrase and try to avoid plagiarism while writing from sources in a foreign language. Its aim is to identify strategies used by students, recognise some features these strategies share, and organise them into categories. This article reports on the first stage of this study of the paraphrasing and plagiarism avoidance strategies used during academic writing tasks in FL, the ultimate aim of the study being to create a scale measuring student's strategic behaviour while paraphrasing.

3. The study

3.1. Participants

A hundred and ten MA students from three public universities in the south of Poland took part in the study. All were second year students in English philology and were in the process of writing their MA dissertations in English.

3.2. Instrument

This study reports on the data acquired via a questionnaire in which students were required to reflect on the paraphrasing and plagiarism avoidance strategies used by them while writing their MA dissertations. The questionnaire consisted of open questions which were formulated in the following way:

> What strategies do you use while paraphrasing and avoiding plagiarism when writing your MA dissertation. Specifically:
>
> 1. What do you do before writing a paraphrase?
>
> 2. What do you do while writing your paraphrase?
>
> 3. What do you do once you have written your paraphrase?
>
> 4. Do you check whether your paraphrase is plagiaristic? If so what do you?

There was also one additional question in the questionnaire: 'Do you have any problems with paraphrasing? If so, what do you find problematic?'. The aim of this question was to gather additional data that would help to contextualise strategies reported by students.

The first three questions were formulated in order to elicit from students information on strategies applied during the first three stages of paraphrasing[3], namely before writing a paraphrase, while writing, and once it has been written. This division of paraphrasing strategies was partially modelled on the division of writing strategies by Petrić and Czárl (2003) into 'Before I start writing an essay in English', 'When writing in English', and 'When revising' and on a taxonomy of writing strategies proposed by De Silva (2010) based on before-writing, while-writing, and after-writing strategies. The fourth question aimed to elicit from students information on whether they check their paraphrasing for potential plagiarism during all three stages of paraphrasing.

---

[3]. The literature does not state that there are three stages of paraphrasing; however, this tripartite model, based on a division of the writing process into planning, translating, and revising (Flower & Hayes, 1980), seemed reasonable to follow as it allows for the analysis of a broader context of paraphrasing by including what happens right before and right after text transformations during paraphrasing.

The students filled in the questionnaire during their classes. Participation in the study was voluntary and the questionnaire anonymous.

3.3. Data analysis

Qualitative analysis was applied in the study in order to investigate strategies reported by students. Students' responses from questionnaires were closely and recursively analysed by the author of the article in order to identify interconnecting categories and dimensions and consequently form a typology (Woods, 2006). Following Yang (2014, p. 80), it may be said that "analytic induction" and "constant comparison" were applied to categorise the strategies reported in the questionnaires.

4. Results

The study identified an array of strategies employed by students when they paraphrase and try to avoid plagiarising. The strategies they apply before writing down a paraphrase are mainly connected with how they read and analyse source materials. Students set goals for their reading, read in a selective way, work on source material using graphic devices, create separate files with excerpts worthy of citing, add their comments to the marked excerpts, and practise paraphrasing. Some analogies may be observed between Plakans's (2009) taxonomy of reading strategies applied during reading-to-write tasks and the strategies reported in this study. As a result, two categories from Plakans's (2009) strategies have been adopted in order to categorise before-writing strategies of paraphrasing, namely 'goal-setting' strategies and 'cognitive strategies' (details are provided in Table 1).

As far as while-writing paraphrasing strategies are concerned, the study showed that these vary from strategies comprising text modifications not going beyond paraphrased excerpts (restating), text modifications comprising mediation of a source text, text transformations going beyond paraphrasing by the addition of comments and conclusions, writing from memory, the use of external resources, to a strategy of giving-up. For details, see Table 2 below.

Table 1. Before-writing paraphrasing strategies

Goal setting	
Planning for thorough understanding	• I try to understand the article thoroughly, it makes paraphrasing easier.
Planning to memorise information from a text	• I read to memorise the most important information.
Deciding to read in a selective way	• I read to focus on the most important things.
Cognitive strategies	
Understanding of a text	• I look for the gist of the whole paragraph. • I underline key words in an excerpt to be paraphrased.
Practising paraphrasing (silently, in one's mind)	• I close my eyes and say it in my own words. • I paraphrase the text in my mind when I read.
Selecting excerpts for paraphrasing by the use of graphic devices	• I put brackets around an excerpt I could use in my thesis. • I highlight excerpts for quotation in one colour and for paraphrasing in the other.
Selecting excerpts for paraphrasing by copying excerpts (into a separate file, into a thesis) from electronic sources for subsequent paraphrasing	• I use books in PDF so I copy some extracts to my thesis and I later paraphrase them. • When I read I create a separate file with the fragments I like.
Notes and comments	• I take notes (on the margin)[4]. • I add my comments to the material I want to put in my dissertation.

Table 2. While-writing paraphrasing strategies

Writing from memory	• I write from memory. • I do not look at the text.
Text transformations (lexical and syntactic)	• I do not resort only to synonym substitution. • I look for synonyms of the key terms • I mix a few sentences, I combine them and keep their sense

---

[4]. The purpose of such behaviour was not given. If these strategies were used for understanding purposes they may be qualified as cognitive, but if notes were made in order to put them into the dissertation then they can be qualified as belonging to mining strategies.

Mediating a source text	• I try to present information in a more simple and a more clear way.
Staying close to the propositional content	• I try to balance my own wording with keeping the sense of the original.
Reaching beyond paraphrasing	• I add my observations and conclusions.
Use of external resources	• I use dictionary with synonyms.
Referencing	• I immediately give source.
Giving up	• If very difficult I turn to quotation • If it is not possible I give up.

The study also aimed to identify strategies once a paraphrase has been written (the third question in the questionnaire) and strategies connected with checking paraphrases for potential plagiarism (the fourth question). The questionnaires showed that for students, these two categories were synonymous, and they therefore provided the same answers to Questions 3 and 4. Most students (70)[5] prioritised the fourth question over the third one and chose to report how they tackled the problem of plagiarism while paraphrasing. Under the third question they simply wrote 'see below', 'see Point 4' etc. Hence this category includes the strategies applied while checking paraphrases for potential plagiarism. As far as this group of strategies is concerned, the study showed that students applied various strategies including 'comparing a paraphrase with the source', strategies connected with checking 'whose voice is speaking' (reporting for intertextual transparency at source level), delaying self-evaluation to get some perspective on the text, using external resources like the Google search engine or free software for text matching, and asking others for advice; for details see Table 3.

There were also some students (11) who said that they did not use any strategies to check whether a paraphrase was plagiaristic as, for them, restating something with their own words automatically meant elimination of any plagiarism potential. As one student wrote: "It is obvious for me – if I used my own words to restate a piece of a text it means it is not plagiaristic. There is no need for checking".

---

5. 70 out of 99 students, as 11 did not report any strategies in the third and fourth question.

Table 3. After-writing paraphrasing strategies

Comparing the text with the source	• Making sure the lexis is different
	• Making sure the syntax is different
	• Making sure the propositional content is the same (It's difficult to say the same thing with different words, you always change something a bit and nuances are lost)
	• Counting words in a row[6] to avoid plagiarism (I make sure that words in a row are not the same)
Checking whether it is clear whose voice is speaking	• I try to make sure that I did not give any impression that this is my opinion.
Delaying self-evaluation	• I wait till the next day – to have a fresh look / I wait a couple of days and then compare my text with a source.
The use of external resources	• I put my paraphrase into Google / I use a programme for text comparison.
Asking others	• I ask my thesis supervisor / I ask others.

Although it was not a primary aim of the study, students were also asked about possible problems with paraphrasing. An attempt to identify some of the problems that students at this level of FL academic writing development might have was rather to set the context for the use of paraphrasing strategies and plagiarism avoidance. The students reported difficulties with paraphrasing arising out of comprehension problems during the pre-writing stage:

> "I sometimes have access only to a sample of a text (the rest is paid), which makes paraphrasing difficult".

> "It's difficult sometimes for me to understand original and that is why my paraphrase may be wrong".

Some pointed to problems with text transformations during the while-writing stage:

---

6. Students reported that they make sure they do not copy more than three or four words in a row into their writing.

> "It is difficult to change the sentence structure".
>
> "Some sentences are impossible to paraphrase".
>
> "There are no synonyms to some concepts – which is difficult to deal with".

As far as the post-writing stage is concerned, students indicated that they are sometimes uncertain whether their paraphrases are properly formulated ("Sometimes I don't know whether it's plagiarism or paraphrase") or have doubts about the originality of their own paraphrasing:

> "I think that my paraphrase may not be original (not that it copies exactly from a source, but somebody else might have paraphrased that piece in a similar way".

5. Discussion

The study allowed to identify a diversity of strategies that are applied by students while paraphrasing source materials in an FL. They can be divided into three groups that mirror the stages of writing, namely the before-writing, while-writing, and after-writing stages. The strategies were reported by second year MA students who were in the second year of writing their MA dissertations, therefore it may be assumed that the reports came from quite experienced writers. The reports also show what strategic behaviours students had developed during their five-year experience of academic writing.

The before-writing paraphrasing strategies used while reading and analysing sources focussed on macro-level understandings with an emphasis on an understanding of the main ideas and memorising key information (for comprehension at a macro or higher level see e.g. Koda, 2004, or Grabe, 2009). These strategies seem to present a global approach to reading which is crucial in efficient paraphrasing and writing from sources (Howard et al., 2010; Shi,

2012) and which has been found to be characteristic for high-scoring students in reading-to-write tasks (Plakans, 2009). It may be contrasted with local text analysis that focusses only on 'good sentences' worth putting in one's writing which is not a recommended approach for academic writing as it often results in patchwriting and plagiarism (Howard et al., 2010).

The study also showed that, while reading, students decide which excerpts to paraphrase and which to quote verbatim. This may partially explain the use of the strategy of 'silent paraphrasing' at a before-writing stage. It may be applied as a testing device via which students discover whether they are able to paraphrase an excerpt successfully or not and consequently impacts their decision whether to quote or to paraphrase (this assumption, however, requires verification by interviews with students).

Adding notes and comments while reading source materials (although at this stage of the study it is not known what exactly the comments concerned) shows that students reflect on and draw inferences from what they read. This strategy may be highly beneficial as inferencing has been identified as crucial in good paraphrasing (Shi, 2012; Yamada, 2003) and adding one's voice to paraphrased excerpts is also crucial in writing as it shows a writer's authorial voice (Abasi & Akbari, 2008) and maturity (Hirvela & Du, 2013).

During writing, apart from strategies strictly connected with text transformations, students also reported numerous strategies that went beyond merely restating what was in the source text. For example, they pointed to a very important aspect of paraphrasing: mediating academic discourse. Students used this strategy to show that they understand a source text and to make a source text understandable for readers. What is more, mediating academic discourse shows students' authority as writers, as they are no longer reporting but transforming a source in order to fit their own writing style and fulfil some rhetorical function.

Students also reported a strategy that is crucial for maintaining intertextual transparency at a propositional level (for details about types of intertextual transparency see Pecorari & Shaw, 2012). It was a strategy of keeping the propositional content of a source which necessitates what students called "balancing rewording with keeping the sense of the original". Finally a strategy of giving up appeared in students' reports. Similarly to Hirvela and Du's (2013) findings, students gave up paraphrasing and resorted to quotation. In Hirvela and Du's (2013) study, this resulted from students' insecurity as writers, their lack of authorial voice, and confusion as to the rhetorical functions of paraphrasing, which may also be true for some participants of this study. On the other hand, as the investigated students of the current study were in the second year of their MA programme and have had some experience in academic writing, such a strategy may be also seen as a sign of students' authority and empowerment as writers. They assess what is possible for them to paraphrase and consciously withdraw from their initial plan of paraphrasing when there might be a chance of violating various aspects of intertextual transparency.

As far as strategies applied while checking paraphrases for potential plagiarism are concerned, students reported resorting to comparison at various textual levels. For example students used a strategy of comparing from a perspective of intertextual transparency at content level as they were aware that rewording bears the risk of changing the propositional content of the source ("nuances are lost"). They also reported having used a strategy of checking the boundaries between their own input into the text and the input of sources. This is vital as students have been found (e.g. Pecorari, 2003, 2008; Pecorari & Shaw, 2012) to blur the borders between sources and their own words. Delaying self-evaluation was also identified among paraphrasing strategies; this seems a highly valuable strategy as it allows to distance oneself from one's own writing and have a fresh look at whether paraphrases are properly formulated. Although students used a variety of strategies to monitor their paraphrases for plagiarism, they also resorted to help from external resources; Google or text matching programmes. On the one hand it may show students' resourcefulness in applying all possible devices to make sure that they are not plagiarising, but on the other hand it may reflect their insecurity about whether their paraphrasing is non-plagiaristic (which was also signalled by students in the 'problems' section of the questionnaire "I am not sure whether it's enough", "There must be someone who paraphrased it in a very similar way"). Students also admitted that they ask others or their supervisor for advice, which may signal their awareness of the complex nature of paraphrasing and the need to take great care in order to paraphrase efficiently.

It should be added that although the strategies reported by students were not verified for their effectiveness in writing from sources, most of them seem worth recommending to students as strategies to enhance their writing from sources, to help to keep the intertextual transparency of their writing, and help them to avoid plagiarism. Just to name a few, conscious reading of sources in order to select excerpts for quoting or paraphrasing, writing down comments and making notes while reading, making sure that propositional content has not been changed as a result of semantic and syntactic modifications, checking whether it is clear for readers whose voice is speaking at that moment, delaying revision, or consulting others in case of doubt – all of these behaviours have the potential of being highly valuable while writing from sources. The strategies identified in this study could be presented to students during academic writing classes for at least the following two reasons: to make students realise that paraphrasing is a complex undertaking that cannot be approached lightly, and to guide them through the process of paraphrasing, right from reading sources up to checking a paraphrase for potential plagiarism.

5.1. Continuation of the study devoted to the questionnaire construction

A think aloud procedure is needed to follow up this part of the study as it would give some insight into the actual application of strategies when paraphrasing source text in an FL. This seems vital, as students' perceptions of the strategies they use while paraphrasing may differ from the actual strategy they use while writing from sources in practice. To extend the study, an analysis of literature on writing strategies is needed in order to identify some further strategic behaviours that might fit into a paraphrasing setting. Finally, a pilot version of a questionnaire investigating paraphrasing strategies while writing from sources needs to be created that might take a form of a Likert scale, similar to the Oxford Strategy Inventory for Language Learning (Oxford, 1990), with the issues to be assessed on a scale ranging from 'never true of me' to 'always true of me'. Consequently, reliability and validity of the instrument needs to be established. In order to verify the reliability of the instrument, a test-rest method (Hatch & Lazaraton, 1991) may be used; the Cronbach alpha coefficient may not be efficient in this case. Following Petrić and Czárl's (2003) rationale for excluding this method from a writing strategies' context, it may be said that internal consistency is appropriate for instruments which are to measure a single underlying construct. As a consequence, internal consistency may be applicable to a specific group of strategies but not to a questionnaire which is a combination of clusters of strategies. As far as the validity of the questionnaire is concerned, its content may be validated by consultations with faculty members, and members of the target population (students). Construct validity could be evaluated by a comparison with theory, as factor analysis may be inadvisable in this case due to problems with interpreting results (Petrić & Czárl, 2003). Response validity may be established via a think aloud procedure in which participants are asked to verbalise their thoughts while filling in a tested questionnaire (Converse & Presser, 1986; Petrić & Czárl, 2003).

5.2. Further studies of paraphrasing strategies

There are many ways this study can be followed up. One path would be to verify paraphrasing strategies in terms of their effectiveness by conducting a survey of the paraphrasing strategies used by highly-rated and low-rated EFL writers or by verifying the use of strategies in terms of the quality of the final product, which in this case would be the quality of students' writing based on the integration of source texts. A closer look at the paraphrasing strategies reported by students shows that they may not be limited exclusively to FL writing. All of them seem potentially applicable to an L1 context. As there are some studies which indicate both differences and similarities between L1 and L2 writing (e.g. Çandarlı, Bayyurt, & Martı, 2015; Silva, 1993; Kobayashi & Rinnert, 2008), it might be interesting to investigate the relationship between the use of paraphrasing strategies in L1 and FL writing and to observe possible interactions between paraphrasing performed in L1 and FL.

6. Conclusion

The aim of this study was to search for strategies that students apply when paraphrasing source texts in an FL and try to avoid plagiarising. The study allowed an array of strategies to be identified that can be categorised into three groups: before-writing paraphrasing strategies, while-writing paraphrasing strategies, and after-writing paraphrasing strategies, which mainly included checking paraphrases for potential plagiarism. The results of the study could have high educational value as the strategies could be presented to students during academic writing classes in order to help them with effective paraphrasing while writing from sources in an FL and to make them realise that paraphrasing in academic writing entails far more than merely restating a source text in their own words.

References

Abasi, A. R., & Akbari, N. (2008). Are we encouraging patchwriting? Reconsidering the role of the pedagogical context in ESL student writers' transgressive intertextuality. *English for Specific Purposes*, 27(3), 267- 284. https://doi.org/10.1016/j.esp.2008.02.001

Bloch, J. (2012). *Plagiarism, intellectual property and the teaching of L2 writing.* Multilingual Matters Limited. https://doi.org/10.21832/9781847696533

Brown, A. L., & Day, J. D. (1983). Macrorules for summarizing texts: the development of expertise. *Journal of Verbal Learning and Verbal Behavior,* 22(1), 1-14. https://doi.org/10.1016/S0022-5371(83)80002-4

Campbell, C. (1990). Writing with others' words: using background reading text in academic compositions. In B. Kroll (Ed.), *Second language writing: research insights for the classroom* (pp. 211-230). Cambridge University Press. https://doi.org/10.1017/CBO9781139524551.018

Çandarlı, D., Bayyurt, Y., & Martı, L. (2015). Authorial presence in L1 and L2 novice academic writing: cross-linguistic and cross-cultural perspectives. *Journal of English for Academic Purposes,* 20, 192-202. https://doi.org/10.1016/j.jeap.2015.10.001

Carson, J. G, & Leki, I. (1993). Introduction. In J. G. Carson & I. Leki (Eds), *Reading in the composition classroom: second language perspectives* (pp. 1-7). Heinle & Heinle.

Cohen, A. (1994). English for academic purposes in Brazil: the use of summary tasks. In C. Hill & K. Parry (Eds), *From testing to assessment: English as an international language* (pp. 174-204). Longman.

Converse, J. M., & Presser, S. (1986). *Survey questions: handcrafting the standardized questionnaire*. Sage Publications. https://doi.org/10.4135/9781412986045

De Silva, K. R. M. (2010). *The impact of writing strategy instruction on EAP students' writing strategy use and writing performance*. Unpublished doctoral dissertation. University of Reading.

Esmaeili, H. (2002). Integrated reading and writing tasks and ESL students' reading and writing performance in an English language test. *Canadian Modern Language Journal, 58*(4), 599-622. https://doi.org/10.3138/cmlr.58.4.599

Flower, L., & Hayes, J. R. (1980). The cognition of discovery: defining a rhetorical problem. *College composition and communication, 31*(1), 21-32.

Grabe, W. (2009). *Reading in a second language. Moving from theory to practice*. Cambridge University Press.

Groom, N. (2000). Attribution and averral revisited: three perspectives on manifest intertextuality in academic writing. In P. Thompson (Ed.), *Patterns and perspectives: insights into EAP writing practice* (pp. 14-25). Reading: Center for Applied Language Studies.

Hatch, E., & Lazaraton, A. (1991). *The research manual. Design and statistics for applied linguistics*. Heinle.

Hirvela, A. (2004). *Connecting reading and writing in second language instruction*. The University of Michigan Press. https://doi.org/10.3998/mpub.23736

Hirvela, A., & Du, Q. (2013). "Why am I paraphrasing?": undergraduate ESL writers; engagement with source-based academic writing and reading. *Journal of English for Academic Purposes, 12*(2), 87-98. https://doi.org/10.1016/j.jeap.2012.11.005

Howard, R. M. (1995). Plagiarism, authorships, and the academic penalty. *College English, 57*(7), 788-806. https://doi.org/10.2307/378403

Howard, R., Serviss, T., & Rodrigue, T. K. (2010). Writing from sources, writing from sentences. *Writing & Pedagogy, 2*(2), 177-192. https://doi.org/10.1558/wap.v2i2.177

Hyland, K. (2002). Activity and evaluation: reporting practices in academic writing. In: J. Flowerdew (Ed.), *Academic discourse* (p.115-130). Longman.

Johns, A. M., & Mayes, P. (1990). An analysis of summary protocols of university students. *Applied Linguistics, 11*(3), 254-271. https://doi.org/10.1093/applin/11.3.253

Keck, C. (2006). The use of paraphrase in summary writing: a comparison of L1 and L2 writers. *Journal of Second Language Writing, 15*(4), 261-278. https://doi.org/10.1016/j.jslw.2006.09.006

Keck, C. (2010). How do university students attempt to avoid plagiarism? A grammatical analysis of undergraduate paraphrasing strategies. *Writing & Pedagogy, 2*(2), 193-222. https://doi.org/10.1558/wap.v2i2.193

Keck, C. (2014). Copying, paraphrasing, and academic writing development: a re-examination of L1 and L2 summarisation practices. *Journal of Second Language Writing, 25*, 4-22. https://doi.org/10.1016/j.jslw.2014.05.005

Kobayashi, H., & Rinnert, C. (2008). Task response and text construction across L1 and L2 writing. *Journal of Second Language Writing, 17*(1), 7-29. https://doi.org/10.1016/j.jslw.2007.08.004

Koda, K. (2004). *Insights into second language reading*. Cambridge Applied Linguistics.

Oxford, R. (1990). *Language learning strategies: what every teacher should know*. Newbury House.

Pecorari, D. (2003). Good and original: plagiarism and patchwriting in academic second-language writing. *Journal of Second Language Writing, 12*(4), 317-345. https://doi.org/10.1016/j.jslw.2003.08.004

Pecorari, D. (2008). *Academic writing and plagiarism: a linguistic analysis*. Continuum.

Pecorari, D., & Shaw, P. (2012). Types of student intertextuality and faculty attitudes. *Journal of Second Language Writing, 21*(2), 149-164. https://doi.org/10.1016/j.jslw.2012.03.006

Petrić, B. (2012). Legitimate textual borrowing: direct quotation in L2 student writing. *Journal of Second Language Writing, 21*(2), 102-117. https://doi.org/10.1016/j.jslw.2012.03.005

Petrić, B., & Czárl, B. (2003). Validating a writing strategy questionnaire. *System, 31*(2), 181-215. https://doi.org/10.1016/S0346-251X(03)00020-4

Phakiti, A. (2003). A closer look at gender and strategy use in L2 reading. *Language Learning, 53*(4), 649-702. https://doi.org/10.1046/j.1467-9922.2003.00239.x

Plakans, L. (2009). The role of reading strategies in integrated L2 writing tasks. *Journal of English for Academic Purposes, 8*(4), 252-266. https://doi.org/10.1016/j.jeap.2009.05.001

Roig, M. (1997). Can undergraduate students determine whether text has been plagiarized? *The Psychological Record, 47*(1), 113-122. https://doi.org/10.1007/BF03395215

Roig, M. (1999). When college students' attempts at paraphrasing become instances of potential plagiarism. *Psychological Reports, 84*(3), 973-982. https://doi.org/10.2466/pr0.1999.84.3.973

Shi, L. (2004). Textual borrowing in second-language writing. *Written Communication, 21*(2), 171-200. https://doi.org/10.1177/0741088303262846

Shi, L. (2012). Rewriting and paraphrasing source texts in second language writing. *Journal of Second Language Writing, 21*(2), 134-148. https://doi.org/10.1016/j.jslw.2012.03.003

Silva, T. (1993). Toward and understanding of the distinct nature of l2 writing. *TESOL Quarterly, 27*(4), 657-677.

Taylor, K. K. (1984). The different summary skills of inexperienced and professional writers. *Journal of Reading, 27*, 691-699.

Thompson, G., & Ye, Y. (1991). Evaluation of the reporting verbs used in academic papers. *Applied Linguistics, 12*(4), 365-82. https://doi.org/10.1093/applin/12.4.365

Wette, R. (2010). Evaluating student learning in a university-level EAP unit on writing using sources. *Journal of Second Language Writing, 19*(3), 158-177. https://doi.org/10.1016/j.jslw.2010.06.002

Woods, P. (2006). *Successful writing for qualitative researchers*. Routledge. https://doi.org/10.4324/9780203001721

Yamada, K. (2003). What prevents ESL/EFL writers from avoiding plagiarism? Analyses of 10 North-American college websites. *System, 31*(2), 247-258. https://doi.org/10.1016/S0346-251X(03)00023-X

Yang, L. (2014). Examining the meditational means in collaborative writing: case studies of undergraduate ESL students in business courses. *Journal of Second Language Writing, 23*, 74-89. https://doi.org/10.1016/j.jslw.2014.01.003

Yang, L., & Shi, L. (2003). Exploring six MBA students' summary writing by introspection. *Journal of English for Academic Purposes, 2*(3), 165-192. https://doi.org/10.1016/S1475-1585(03)00016-X

7 Rethinking study abroad and intercultural competence

Chesla Ann Lenkaitis[1]

Abstract

Due to competing demands of university students, short-term study abroad trips are on the rise (Lewis & Niesenbaum, 2005; NAFSA, 2003, 2019). The present study is the only study that has explored a trip of less than one week and the ways in which L2 participants have developed their intercultural competence daily. Like in Allen (2010), this study was small in scale, since only two second language (L2) learners of Spanish studied abroad. In addition, this study used Merriam's (1998) case study framework to illuminate the case of two L2 learners and their short-term five-day study abroad experience. Analyses of surveys and Deardorff's (2012) Intercultural Competence (IC) self-reflection, coupled with field notes, revealed that participants' daily fluctuations of up to 18.7% did occur, thus demonstrating IC's dynamicity (Deardorff, 2012). Not only is a short-term study abroad of less than one week practical for university students, but this study also suggested that a non-traditional short-term study abroad can be a valuable tool to an L2 learner's IC development.

Keywords: foreign language higher education, intercultural competence, qualitative research, second language teaching and learning, study abroad.

1. Binghamton University, New York, United States; lenkaitis@binghamton.edu

How to cite this chapter: Lenkaitis, C. A. (2019). Rethinking study abroad and intercultural competence. In B. Loranc-Paszylk (Ed.), *Rethinking directions in language learning and teaching at university level* (pp. 137-163). Research-publishing.net. https://doi.org/10.14705/rpnet.2019.31.895

Chapter 7

1. Introduction

Cultures is one of the five standards for language learning (ACTFL, 1996, 2015), and having the ability to study abroad is advantageous in order to facilitate language learning and develop IC, the ability to interact in an L2 effectively and appropriately (Bennett & Bennett, 2004), and increase knowledge of the L2 culture (Anderson, Hubbard, & Lawton, 2015; Anderson & Lawton, 2011). In addition to being valued by universities (Anderson et al., 2015), study abroad makes a job applicant more desirable for employment (Franklin, 2010; Hart Research Association, 2010; Kumaravadivelu, 2008).

However, due to course demands, scheduling conflicts, and the increase in travel expenses (Lewis & Niesenbaum, 2005; NAFSA, 2003), a shorter-term study abroad trip can be an alternative to a semester or year-long one. This type of experience can still be valuable to university students (Brubaker, 2007; Chieffo & Griffiths, 2009; Donnelly-Smith, 2009; Kartoshkina, Chieffo, & Kang, 2013) and give L2 learners "significant exposure to the target language and culture" (Savage & Hughes, 2014, p. 118). Typically, a short-term study abroad can last as short as a few weeks to as long as a few months (Kartoshkina et al., 2013).

Although there are studies that have examined short-term study abroad (Brubaker, 2007; Czerwionka, Artamonova, & Barbosa, 2014; Donnelly-Smith, 2009; Jackson, 2011; Lewis & Niesenbaum, 2005; Shiri, 2015; Williams, 2009), the current study is the only one that has explored a study abroad trip of less than a week and the ways in which L2 learners develop their IC during its duration.

2. Literature review

2.1. Study abroad

Due to the increase in globalization and interconnectedness of our world, many students have been encouraged to study abroad (O'Rourke & Williamson, 2002). Collaborative learning is valued and in many ways learning has become international and "gone global" (Kahn & Agnew, 2017, p. 53). In study abroad experiences, L2 learners develop knowledge of the L2 country and culture (Chieffo & Griffiths, 2004; Shiri, 2015) and become more interculturally competent as they are able to effectively communicate in a variety of situations abroad (Bennett & Bennett, 2004; Shiri, 2015).

Having access to native-speakers is crucial during any study-abroad program not only for language development but also for cultural growth (Castañeda & Zirger, 2011). Since short-term study abroad programs are just that, short, it is important that such programs have guidance (Brubaker, 2007) and direct cultural engagement since there is limited time for interactions to occur organically (Ingram, 2005). With these interactions, coupled with data collected before and after a study abroad experience (Czerwionka et al., 2014), students have shown to have meaningful contact with native speakers that support language and cultural development (Castañeda & Zirger, 2011; Wang, 2010).

In the past, short-term study abroad has been considered less valuable than programs that lasted a semester or a year (Davidson, 2007; Dwyer & Peters, 2004; Freed, 1990; Ingram, 2005). However, the number of those traveling for shorter time frames has been on the rise (Institute of International Education, 2018), and studies have shown that short-term study abroad can provide valuable experiences to students and support their development (Castañeda & Zirger, 2011; Félix-Brasdefer & Hasler-Barker, 2015; Levine & Garland, 2015; Serrano, Llanes, & Tragant, 2016; Shiri, 2015). Some university coursework even includes a short-term study abroad component during which students can work on interdisciplinary projects over a two-week period (Lewis & Niesenbaum, 2005).

According to NAFSA (2019), although there was an increase of students from the United States who studied abroad for credit in the 2016-2017 academic year, the total number of students only represented 1.6% of university students and only approximately 10% of graduates from the United States. Of these study abroad experiences, those lasting eight weeks or less have shown to be on the rise (Jackson, 2011). According to the Institute of International Education's

(2018) Open Doors report, out of the total 332,727 university students from the United States who studied abroad in 2016-2017, summer term programs had the highest percentage of participants with 38.5% while semester programs came in with the second highest number at 30.7%. Of these 300,000+ students, almost 62% had a study abroad experience of eight weeks or less. This was an increase from 58.1% in 2010-2011, when data of this duration was first reported. Of these programs of eight weeks or less, approximately 17% of these students have participated in study abroad experiences lasting less than two weeks. This percentage has also been on the rise from 11.6% in 2010-2011[2].

2.2. Intercultural competence

There are several IC frameworks and many perspectives on the IC construct (Moeller & Nugent, 2014; Schulz, 2007; Stemler, Imada, & Sorkin, 2014). Bennett's (1993) developmental model of intercultural sensitivity offers a framework that explains how individual thoughts and feelings about culture create cultural difference. As a person becomes less ethnocentric and more ethnorelative, in turn, he/she becomes more interculturally competent. Byram's (1997) seminal work details the necessary attitudes, knowledge, and skills to successfully interact with people of an L2 culture.

Expanding upon Byram's (1997) work, Deardorff's (2006) process model of IC focuses on (1) attitudes, (2) knowledge and comprehension, (3) skills, (4) internal outcomes, and (5) external outcomes. Theoretically, the first three elements of attitudes, knowledge and comprehension, and skills lead to an individual's internal outcomes. In turn, external outcomes are developed and visible to others in intercultural situations (Deardorff, 2006, p. 2012).

2.3. Theoretical framework

Even though some consensus has been reached about how to define IC (Deardorff, 2006), there are a variety of ways to assess IC and to date, it is difficult to say

---

2. Since no detailed information about January term programs was in the data, they were not factored into the summary of the programs of less than two weeks.

which is the best assessment (Braskamp, Braskamp, & Merrill, 2009; Stebleton, Soria, & Cherney, 2012-2013).

For this study, the researcher chose to utilize Deardorff's (2012) IC self-reflection, which was developed from her process model (Deardorff, 2006). Not only does this self-reflection center around 15 items that are critical in developing IC, but it also has not been used to assess students during a study abroad experience. In the first part of this self-reflection, the participant is asked to rate him/herself on 15 categories of IC on a five-point Likert scale (1=poor; 5=very high) while in the second, he/she is asked to elaborate on situations that required one or more of the 15 categories of IC.

Deardorff's (2012) 15 categories include the following: (1) respect, (2) openness, (3) tolerance for ambiguity, (4) flexibility, (5) curiosity and discovery, (6) withholding judgment, (7) cultural self-awareness/understanding, (8) understanding others' worldviews, (9) culture-specific knowledge, (10) sociolinguistic awareness, (11) skills to listen, observe, and interpret, (12) skills to analyze, evaluate, and relate, (13) empathy, (14) adaptability, and (15) communication skills. According to Deardorff's (2006) process model, respect, openness, tolerance for ambiguity, withholding judgment, and curiosity and discovery fall under the attitudes component. The categories of cultural self-awareness/understanding, understanding others' worldviews, culture-specific knowledge, and sociolinguistic awareness fall under knowledge and comprehension, while the skills to listen, observe, and interpret, and skills to analyze, evaluate, and relate are grouped under skills. Internal outcomes include flexibility, empathy, and adaptability, and external outcomes encompass communication skills.

Although Deardorff's (2012) 15 categories can be grouped under her process model (Deardorff, 2006), they are not defined in much detail. Therefore, for this study, the researcher adapted definitions from Lenkaitis, Calo, and Venegas-Escobar (2019)[3].

---

3. The adapted definitions are available upon request from the author.

2.4. Research questions

Due to the increasing number of students who are participating in short-term study abroad and the importance of becoming interculturally competent in our globalized world, this study explored the ways in which participants' IC developed daily over a 5-day study abroad trip. Not only did this study use an assessment that has not been studied for study abroad, but it also examined a duration that has not been researched. Therefore, this study will answer the following Research Questions (RQs):

- RQ1: Is a five-day study abroad experience sufficient to improve IC?

- RQ2: In what IC categories, as per Deardorff (2012), do participants show growth?

- RQ3: In what ways do participants' perceptions change over the course of a five-day study abroad?

3. Methodology

3.1. Participants

After having participated in a Collaborative Online International Learning (COIL) project that partnered L2 learners of Spanish from a university in the USA with L2 learners of English from a university in Mexico, there was an opportunity for students from the USA to travel to Mexico. Two L2 learners of Spanish applied for this short-term study abroad experience and both were chosen to travel to Mexico with their course instructor to meet and interact with personnel from the partnering institution.

Both participants were registered students of a first semester intermediate Spanish course during the time of the COIL project. Participant 1 (P1) was 19 years old and Participant 2 (P2) was 20 years old. Neither participant had studied abroad before and like in Allen's (2010) small-scale study of six intermediate-level students, this study was small in scale because only two L2 learners of Spanish studied abroad. In addition, this study used Merriam's (1998) case study framework to illuminate the case of two L2 learners and the short-term study abroad experience that they each participated in over the course of five days.

Students in study abroad programs are often not prepared to maximize their learning (Goldoni, 2015) and time while abroad (Jackson, 2008). Students may only be able to experience superficial cultural experiences since they have the tendency to remain in an L1 peer group or treat the experience as a vacation (Allen, 2010). However, through the structured and adult-accompanied itinerary that the L2 learners kept, the researcher was able to guarantee that participants interacted with native speakers, limited their use of English and maintained conversations in Spanish, and had meaningful cultural opportunities for L2 learner development (He, Lundgren, & Pynes, 2017, Shively, 2015; Tomaš, Farrelly, & Haslam, 2008). Activities included tours of the partnering institution, dinner at traditional Mexican restaurants, visits to national parks, and time spent in the homes of a faculty member and student.

3.2. Procedure

Due to the fact that having multiple measures is crucial to assess development during a study abroad experience (Anderson & Lawton, 2011; Hammer, Bennett, & Wiseman, 2003; He et al., 2017), several were taken during this study. Prior to traveling to Mexico, participants completed Deardorff's (2012) IC self-reflection[4]. Participants rated themselves on a five-point Likert-scale (1=poor; 5=very high) for each of Deardorff's (2012) 15 categories of IC listed and then had the opportunity to write about situations where they used one or more of the 15 categories of IC. In addition, background information was gathered from both participants in a ten-question survey via surveymonkey.com, including a language skills self-assessment (1=not proficient at all; 10=very proficient).

---

4. The pre-survey questions are available upon request from the author.

Chapter 7

During the trip, participants completed Deardorff's (2012) IC self-reflection daily[5]. Participants also reflected on their experiences while in Mexico each day in a six-question survey. They answered questions about their daily experience in Mexico and aspects of the Mexican culture and language. Participants commented on the aspects of the Mexican culture that they liked the best as well as those that they liked the least. Finally, upon returning to the United States, participants completed Deardorff's (2012) IC self-reflection as well as a seven-question post-survey[6], similar in structure to that of the pre-survey, including a language skills self-assessment.

In conjunction with these daily assessments, the participants' Spanish professor had the opportunity to observe the two L2 learners in a variety of situations; both formal and informal. Her field notes of these two participants were also used for analysis (Jackson, 2011).

4. Results

4.1. Deardorff's (2012) IC self-reflection

4.1.1. 15 categories of IC self-rating

Since there were 15 categories listed that participants rated themselves on and each rating was on a five-point Likert scale, there was a possible total 75 points (15 aspects times five). Results showed that both participants improved their IC score from before to after the short-term study abroad experience. However, these self-ratings also indicated that IC is distinct to each individual person (Deardorff, 2012). Table 1 details participants' self-ratings of Deardorff's (2012) 15 categories before, during, and after travel using the scale, as given by Deardorff (2012) of one (poor) to five (very high).

---

5. The daily questions are available upon request from the author.
6. The post-survey questions are available upon request from the author.

Table 1. Deardorff's (2012) 15 categories of IC self-rating before and after travel[7]

	Pre		Day 1		Day 2		Day 3		Day 4		Day 5		Post		Average	
	P1	P2	P1	P2	P1	P2	P1	P2	P1	P2	P1	P2	P1	P2	P1	P2
Respect	4	5	3	5	4	5	3	5	4	4	4	5	4	5	3.7	4.9
Openness	3	5	3	5	4	5	3	5	4	5	4	5	4	5	3.6	5
Tolerance for ambiguity	3	4	2	4	3	4	3	4	4	3	3	0	3	4	3	3.3
Flexibility	3	5	4	4	4	5	3	5	4	0	3	5	3	5	3.4	4.1
Curiosity and discovery	5	5	5	5	5	5	4	5	5	5	5	5	5	5	4.9	5
Withholding judgment	3	5	2	4	2	4	1	4	3	4	3	3	3	5	2.6	4.1
Cultural self-awareness/ understanding	3	4	3	4	3	4	2	4	4	4	4	0	3	5	3.3	3.6
Understanding other's worldviews	4	4	3	5	3	4	2	4	4	4	4	5	4	5	3.6	4.4
Cultural specific-knowledge	4	2	4	3	3	4	3	4	3	4	3	5	4	4	3.6	3.7
Socio-linguistic awareness	4	4	3	0	3	3	2	4	3	4	4	0	3	4	3.3	2.7
Skills to listen, observe, and interpret	4	4	5	4	5	3	5	4	5	4	5	4	5	4	4.9	3.9
Skills to analyze, evaluate, and relate	3	5	5	4	5	4	5	4	5	4	5	5	5	5	4.7	4.4
Empathy	3	5	4	5	3	5	4	5	4	5	4	5	3	5	3.6	5
Adaptability	4	4	3	4	3	4	2	5	3	5	3	5	3	5	3	4.6
Communication skills	4	3	3	4	2	4	1	3	3	3	2	5	3	5	2.6	3.9
Total (out of 75)	54	64	52	60	52	63	48	65	58	58	56	57	55	71	53.6	62.6

---

7. If a zero is listed, the participant did not rate himself/herself on this aspect of IC on the given day.

Chapter 7

For example, out of 75, P1 rated himself 54 on all aspects of IC before leaving for Mexico and upon returning to the United States, a 55. Therefore, as a percentage, P1's rating increased a mere 1% from 72% to 73.3%. Meanwhile P2's rating before the study abroad was 64 out of 75 and after it increased seven points to 71. Therefore, before the study abroad she rated herself 85.3% on IC while after she rated herself 94.7%.

When specifically looking at daily fluctuations, the data revealed that both positive and negative fluctuations from -9.3% to +18.7% emerged, thus showing the variability of IC and the way in which L2 learners' feelings can vacillate when it comes to their IC development. Increases were noted in certain categories on certain days, while participants indicated decreases on other days. Also, some categories remained consistent over a few days. Table 2 shows the percentage of IC fluctuation that occurred daily.

Table 2. Overall intercultural competence daily fluctuations in terms of percentage

Pre		Day 1		Day 2		Day 3		Day 4		Day 5		Post		Overall (from pre to post)	
P1	P2	P1	P2	P1	P2	P1	P2	P1	P2	P1	P2	P1	P2	P1	P2
54	64	52	60	52	63	48	65	58	58	56	57	55	71	54→55	64→71
-	-	-2.7	-5.3	0.0	+4.0	-5.3	+2.7	+13.2	-9.3	-2.7	-1.3	-1.3	+18.7	+1.3	+9.3

4.1.2. Open-ended response on IC

Participant 1

Prior to the short-term travel, P1 mentioned "keeping an open mind is crucial" and "using an objective lense [sic]… will allow me to remove what ever [sic] prejudices I may have about foreign cultures". Although P1 mentioned that he needed to "work on organically communicating", he also mentioned the following on Day 1: "I find it hard (sometimes) to contribute when I am not directly spoken to… I feel that I am making progress". More than once throughout the short-term study abroad, P1 mentioned comments that included him saying he needs to not be afraid to make mistakes and that he needs to leave his "comfort zone" (Day 1), put himself "out there" (Day 2), and on Day 5 to become "a contributor more". Even though he indicated that he had "envy" because others were able to "enter conversation so easily", he also wrote, "I find my listening comprehension increasing a lot". Nonetheless, by the last full day in Mexico, P1 started leaving his "comfort zone" more as he became more confident in trying to communicate with the Mexican people and commented that "I try to use Span[ish], but for vital info, I still need English". Upon returning to the United States, P1 commented, "[g]aging [sic] the situation helped my interactions. Processing what I'd like to say first helped, but led to me 'over thinking' my spanish [sic]. Being culturally aware means more than just speaking but also interacting".

Participant 2

P2 indicated in her open-ended response prior to the short-term study abroad that "it is important to first observe someone from another culture, to learn more and to see how it would be appropriate to talk to them". She proceeds to comment that she "would really like to observe to learn the culture and see how the other culture interacts with itself and with others like myself".

On Day 1, P2 commented that

> "I'm still learning culture-specific knowledge about Mexico, however, I find more now that I am less afraid to ask what something means if I don't understand. This is because I obviously need to understand whomever I'm talking with in order to learn/gain more cultural-specific knowledge".

Throughout the trip, P2 mentions specific situations and makes connections between the L1 and L2 cultures. She writes,

> "I try to imagine how I look as I'm doing something so I can be self-aware and not make any alarming facial expressions when talking to someone from another culture. I usually just try to reflect/mirror what whomever I'm talking to is doing".

On the last evening in Mexico, P2 reflected on her experience and understood that she may have misinterpreted some things and made a realization that interactions may be different based on people's backgrounds by writing,

> "[i]n hindsight, I may have thought something was said a little maliciously or with offense because I was nervous about whether or not I understood everything or whether or not I would be able to respond well. Also, I recognize that we spent time primarily with mid-upper class, educated people. I believe this factor is similar reflection on the people that we've met to how our socio-economic status affects us in the U.S.".

Upon returning to the United States, P2 reflected on her experience and what she plans on doing post-study abroad. She even incorporated Spanish at the end of her open-ended response to note that her observation was obvious. She wrote,

> "I became more appropriate in my reactions by watching how they responded to me. I plan to further develop my intercultural competence by video chatting… to learn more about their culture. Also, I plan on learning more vocabulary. I found that I really couldn't understand the meaning of a phrase if it was with vocabulary that I didn't know… obvio".

4.2. Researcher-created pre- and post-surveys

4.2.1. Language skills self-assessment

Participant self-ratings before and after their short-term study abroad, using a ten-point scale (1=not proficient at all; 5=very proficient) on the four language skills – speaking, reading, listening, and writing – showed some changed. Table 3 summarizes the participant self-ratings.

Table 3. Language skills self-assessment before and after travel

	Participant 1			Participant 2		
	Before	After	Change	Before	After	Change
Speaking	5	6	+1	6	7	+1
Reading	6	7	+1	7	7.5	+0.5
Listening	5	5	0	6	6	0
Writing	7	6	-1	8	8	0

4.2.2. Study abroad objectives

Upon being asked what they wanted to gain from the trip, both participants indicated that they wanted to improve their language and culture skills. P1 mentioned that he wanted to expose himself in a country "where English is not the primary language used", while P2 wrote that she wanted "an increased ability to speak Spanish, a heightened understanding for the Mexican culture and an appreciated group of new long-term friends". When reflecting about the trip, P1 stated that "[y]es I gained a lot from this trip. Being exposed to the language 24/7... developed my Spanish skills greatly". P2 indicated that she "learned so much about the culture and got to experience the land and people there".

4.3. Researcher-created daily surveys

4.3.1. Coding

In addition to the open-ended response as per Deardorff's (2012) IC self-reflection, participants also answered researcher-created questions daily. Open-ended answers were coded both deductively and inductively by units of instances. An instance consisted of a word, a phrase, a sentence, or group of sentences (Bohinski[8] & Leventhal, 2015), since intercultural learning or development is not quantified for a specific word count.

---

8. Prior to a name change due to marriage, Chesla used her maiden name, Bohinski, for publications.

Data were independently coded by the two coders. A 92.2% agreement rate (Kappa=0.70 with $p<0.001$) was achieved after initial coding. Subsequently, coders worked together to reconcile the remaining differences.

4.3.2. Deductive approach

All open-ended responses were coded using a deductive approach, using Deardorff's (2012) 15 categories of IC. In this way, the researcher was able to explore participants' IC and changes that occurred before, during, and after the short-term study abroad and use this data to complement the participants' self-ratings on Deardorff's (2012) 15 categories.

The results indicated that participants concentrated on specific aspects of their IC in their written responses. Not only did they focus on being open to the L2 culture (openness), but their understanding of the L2's worldviews (understanding other's worldviews) was the another highly coded category. Four categories (flexibility, curiosity and discovery, cultural-specific knowledge, and sociolinguistic awareness) were coded just once. Table 4 shows deductive coding examples while Table 5 details the deductive coding results for the open-ended researcher-created open-ended survey questions.

Table 4. Deductive coding examples[9]

Respect	"I appreciate and recognize the generosity of those hosting us, but I already knew the Mexicans are giving people to those they trust" (P2).
Openness	"Overall, I am trying to speak as much Spanish as possible" (P2).
Tolerance for ambiguity	"More often than not I will not say anything (or refrain from conversing) instead of speaking English" (P1).
Flexibility	"I liked speaking with [removed for anonymity]'s sister because she made me feel comfortable speaking. I also am more comfortable talking to workers, but only if I plan out what I want to say" (P2).

9. Researcher's English translations are given in parentheses.

Curiosity and discovery	"There's also more personality given in small talk between strangers – for example, if a stranger asks if they may pass, a [M]exicano might be more likely to say, 'Sí, claro que sí' (Yes, of course) instead of just, 'Sí' ¿Entiendes? (Yes, do you understand?)" (P2).
Withholding judgment	"I feel like I can pass judgement quickly" (P1).
Cultural self-awareness/ understanding	"Being more expressive as well helped my interactions because I find the Mexicans use so much more facial expressions/energy in conversation than Americans do…" (P2).
Understanding other's worldviews	"They are very laid back about being in the 'here and now'. There is no rush to stop what is going on" (P2).
Cultural specific-knowledge	"Also, I feel that I am missing a solid 'base' of Spanish knowledge" (P1).
Sociolinguistic awareness	"Being more expressive as well helped my interactions" (P2).
Skills to listen, observe, and interpret	"I find it easier to 'decipher' the accents" (P1).
Skills to analyze, evaluate, and relate	"They have all very similar views on respect, humor, and many similar idioms that sometimes they don't even know from where they originated – just like how we don't know where ours came from all the time" (P2).
Empathy	"For example, a man on the boat was holding a baby, and I wanted to watch her, so I made sure to be smiling as I was watching her to show that I was happy to be watching her make bubbles in her mouth and look overly-surprised, but to also let her parents not be alarmed that I was just starting at their baby. I always try to think, in every scenario, from a perspective outside my own or, at least, I try to imagine how I look as I'm doing something so I can be self-aware and not make any alarming facial expressions when talking to someone from another culture" (P2).
Adaptability	"I usually just try to reflect/mirror what whomever I'm talking to is doing" (P2).
Communication skills	"I need to develop my communication skills by 'putting myself out there'" (P1).

Chapter 7

Table 5. Deductive coding results as per Deardorff's (2012) 15 categories over the five-day study abroad

	Day 1		Day 2		Day 3		Day 4		Day 5		Total for 5 days	
	P1	P2	P1	P2	P1	P2	P1	P2	P1	P2	P1	P2
Respect	1	3	2	0	2	0	1	2	1	1	7	6
Openness	5	3	5	0	1	1	1	0	2	1	14	5
Tolerance for ambiguity	3	0	0	0	2	0	1	2	1	2	7	4
Flexibility	0	0	0	0	0	1	0	0	0	0	0	1
Curiosity and discovery	0	0	0	0	0	0	0	0	0	1	0	1
Withholding judgment	1	1	3	1	1	2	1	2	3	0	9	6
Cultural self-awareness/ understanding	0	2	2	2	0	0	0	0	1	0	3	4
Understanding other's worldviews	1	1	2	4	1	1	3	2	4	0	11	8
Cultural specific-knowledge	0	0	0	0	1	0	0	0	0	0	1	0
Sociolinguistic awareness	0	1	0	0	0	0	0	0	0	0	0	1
Skills to listen, observe, and interpret	1	1	1	1	1	1	0	0	1	1	4	4
Skills to analyze, evaluate, and relate	1	0	0	0	0	1	0	0	0	1	1	2
Empathy	0	0	0	2	0	0	0	0	0	2	0	4
Adaptability	0	3	0	1	0	0	0	0	0	0	0	4
Communication skills	2	3	1	0	0	2	1	0	0	1	4	6
Total in each category per day	15	18	16	11	9	9	8	8	13	10	61	56

4.3.3. Inductive approach

In addition to coding with Deardorff's (2012) 15 categories of IC, an inductive approach was also used. From patterns that emerged from the data, the researcher created positive, negative, and reflective coding categories. Both the positive and negative categories had three sub-categories: (1) difference between cultures, (2) confidence and/or motivation (or lack thereof), and (3) language skills.

Therefore, if coded as positive, the comment showed that the participant: (1) noted a positive difference between the L1 and L2 cultures, (2) improved his/her confidence and/or became more proactive to learn the L2, and (3) improved his/her language skills. Conversely, if coded as negative, the comment showed that the participant: (1) noted a negative difference between the L1 and L2 cultures, (2) had doubts in his/her abilities and became demotivated, and (3) faced difficulties with their language skills. If coded as reflective, the comment indicated a reflection, thought, idea, or opinion that a participant mentioned regarding his/her experience.

Out of the 166 responses that were coded, almost 50% were positive, approximately 22% were negative, and about 30% indicated participants being reflective of their experience. Table 6 lists inductive coding examples while Table 7 indicates results for the open-ended daily survey questions.

Table 6. Inductive coding examples

Positive	
Difference in cultures	"The food is also incredible, different but good" (P1).
Confidence and/or motivation	"I also am more comfortable talking to workers, but only if I plan out what I want to say" (P2).
Language skills	"My comfort in speaking has increased and I have learned some new items" (P2).
Negative	
Difference in cultures	"Sometimes there is a gap between our culture when it comes to working extra on the weekends, holidays, etc" (P1).
Doubt and/or demotivation	"I envy [taken out for anonymity] because they can enter conversation so easily" (P1).
Language skills	"It is hard to stick to Spanish in situations where I feel I cannot be able to explain myself or be understood well in Spanish. I revert to English when I have difficulty saying what I want to in Spanish. I do not want to sound 'unintelligent' by not using proper grammar" (P2).
Reflective	"Being slightly more conservative in some (underlined) social contexts is like taking a break from my fast-paced day-to-day life" (P1).

Chapter 7

Table 7. Inductive coding results as per researcher-created categories over the five-day study abroad

	Day 1		Day 2		Day 3		Day 4		Day 5		Total for 5 days	
	P1	P2	P1	P2	P1	P2	P1	P2	P1	P2	P1	P2
Positive	9	13	10	11	7	7	6	2	7	9	39	43
• Difference in cultures	2	5	4	6	3	1	3	3	5	5	17	20
• Confidence and/ or motivation	6	3	5	0	3	4	3	0	2	2	19	9
• Language skills	1	5	1	5	1	2	0	0	0	2	3	14
Negative	6	4	3	1	6	6	2	4	4	1	21	16
• Difference in cultures	1	1	2	0	12	0	1	2	3	0	9	3
• Doubt and/or demotivation	1	1	0	1	1	1	0	0	0	0	2	3
• Language skills	4	2	1	0	3	5	1	2	1	1	10	10
Reflective	8	4	3	7	2	4	4	2	4	9	21	26

4.4. Researcher field notes

Although P1 was very motivated to improve his speaking skills, he rarely took the initiative to speak on his own, but rather only when spoken to. For example, during an hour drive to visit a state park, it was apparent that P1 did not take the initiative to speak on his own, but rather only answered questions when asked. Nonetheless, by the end of the study abroad experience, it was apparent through the researcher's observations that his skills had improved. Researcher field notes indicated that this L2 learner was taking the initiative to use Spanish during the last evening in Monterrey when he was celebrating Mexican Independence Day.

However, P2 was not afraid to ask questions and engage in the target language. For example, in the same road trip to the state park, P2 spoke freely and made conversation for the entire trip and was asking questions so she could practice her Spanish. Not only during this activity, but throughout the five-day trip, she consistently wrote down new phrases and vocabulary in a notebook to review.

Field notes indicated that she incorporated them in conversation afterward and utilized them correctly. In addition to communication skills development, both participants had the opportunity to interact with the Mexican people daily. Because of these interactions, it was obvious that both participants made connections between the L2 and L1 culture and became more culturally aware.

5. Discussion

To answer RQ1, results suggested that a five-day study abroad experience can contribute to improve IC. Not only did overall IC results increase for each learner, but also results confirmed that IC is dynamic and changes daily (Deardorff, 2012), as each participant had daily fluctuations across Deardorff's (2012) 15 categories. For instance, in response to RQ3, P1 rated himself a four for communication skills prior to leaving for Mexico, but on Day 1 a three. At his lowest, on Day 3, he rated himself a one, but upon returning to the United States, his rating improved to a three. In this same category, P2 rated herself a three prior to the short-term study abroad. However, while in Mexico and after the experience, her rating was at a five. In addition to these self-ratings, the deductive coding of daily open-ended survey questions showed IC's dynamicity as the number of instances of coded instances varied by day and by participant (see Table 5).

To further answer RQ1, in addition to IC development, data from the inductive coding also suggested that a short-term study abroad can be of great value to L2 students (Castañeda & Zirger, 2011; Levine & Garland, 2015; Shiri, 2015). The overwhelming positive experience that students indicated in their open-ended responses, coupled with the self-ratings and research field notes, suggested that a short-term study abroad is beneficial for L2 students. It is important to remember that a short-term study abroad of this length, like any other short-term study abroad experience, should be structured to give L2 learners opportunities to interact with L2 native speakers (Castañeda & Zirger, 2011; Wang, 2010). For example, in this study, both participants of this study had a variety of daily opportunities to interact with native speakers on an individual basis. The only time that L2 participants were not in close contact with L2 native speakers is when they were in the hotel, which consisted of time for sleeping and showering. Apart from these activities, both participants' schedules were packed with numerous daily activities at the partnering institution or with staff, faculty, and students of the partnering institution in Mexico and its surrounding areas.

To answer RQ2 and RQ3, although participants had these fluctuations, it was evident that both participants were developing aspects of their IC through the five-day study abroad. The comments written by participants showed that their communication skills developed and both participants eventually became more confident in using their Spanish skills with native speakers. For example, P1 indicated the value of communication and that he was finding it is "easier" to communicate in certain situations. Results also revealed that the aspects of IC work together and usually don't develop in isolation, which further confirms the ever-changing nature of IC (Deardorff, 2012). During the trip, both participants commented on situations where they were both acquiring components of IC and having difficulties. From researcher field notes, it was evident that P2 felt more confident in trying to communicate with the Mexican people and utilized Spanish energetically in all situations. However, as evidenced in his daily survey, P1, trying to "formulize... [sic] phrased/ideas before speaking", had a harder time leaving his "comfort zone".

Throughout the trip, due to the structured itinerary (Brubaker, 2007; He et al., 2017; Shively, 2015; Tomaš et al., 2008), both participants had a variety of opportunities to interact with the Mexican people and the Spanish language (Castañeda & Zirger, 2011; Wang, 2010). When analyzing the data, the daily experiences of each participant as well as his/her individual developmental processes influenced the self-ratings. By sharing their insights, participants showed that they developed their IC through their daily interactions. However, it was interesting to note that although participants commented on specific experiences and noted progress in certain aspects, they may have not rated themselves accordingly. For example, P1 noted on Day 3 in an open-ended question that his listening skills were improving, which is a part of communication skills, but rated himself at his lowest on this same day. Furthermore, there were a few instances where P2 neglected to rate herself on certain aspects. Not only does this confirm that multiple measures are key while studying abroad (Anderson & Lawton, 2011; Hammer et al., 2003; He et al., 2017), but also that one IC assessment is also needed to evaluate the dynamicity of this construct (Deardorff, 2009; Lenkaitis et al., in press).

Although there were only two L2 participants that took part in this short-term study abroad, the researcher did not see this small sample size as a hurdle, but rather was confident that the study would yield meaningful data. Since this was the first study focusing on this length of short-term study abroad, the groundwork laid by this case study provided a basis for future studies. Being able to concentrate on a case study (Merriam, 1998) for these two students during this experience illustrated that more study must be done in this under researched field.

In the future, having a larger sample size will be beneficial to generalize results, but the researcher does realize that a larger sample size for this type of study abroad will only be possible when this length of trip is regularly made available to a greater number of L2 learners. Nonetheless, using the design that was implemented by the researcher that included a variety of structured activities and data collection that included daily surveys and field notes, should be used as it was beneficial and contributed greatly to the present study.

6. Conclusions

IC is a part of the L2 learning process that must be taken into consideration. It is important that L2 learners develop this competence so that they can appropriately and effectively communicate in the L2. Although work can be done on individual different aspects of IC, it is important that instructors and students remember that not one aspect develops in isolation from others. All components of IC work together. Using an internally-developed tool (Kartoshkina et al., 2013; Levine & Garland, 2015) or providing students with details on every category may be helpful to conceptualize all that makes up IC. In addition to learning about cultural norms in the classroom, L2 students must take accountability for their own learning and be put into situations where they can utilize their target language. Participating in activities where L2 learners are supported by faculty from partnering institutions is key to ensure target language utilization. Furthermore, when participating in a short-term study abroad, it should be purposefully packed so that there are ample opportunities to interact with the L2 and its culture in authentic ways.

Although this study's data showed that participants rated themselves as high as a five in some of Deardorff's (2012) 15 categories, having the opportunity to interact with native speakers in the L2 culture is invaluable. After navigating through real-life situations, these ratings changed based on participants' experiences. The study revealed that while L2 learners may believe that they have developed IC from learning about the L2 culture in their L1 culture, only after experiencing the L2 firsthand will L2 learners truly realize that IC is more than meets the eye. The intricacies that exist in an L2 culture only come to life when faced with interacting with native speakers in real-life situations. Therefore, rethinking study abroad to a structured short-term experience is of great value to develop IC. It is a practical alternative for university students to meaningfully interact with native speakers of the L2 in a variety of contexts.

Acknowledgements

In carrying out this study, the author received assistance from colleagues who deserve her thanks: Eric E. Backlund, Thomas Burke, Salvador Venegas Escobar, John Fowler, Brenda Ivonne García Portillo, Katherine Krebs, Antonio Sobejano-Morán, and Tianhui Zhang.

References

ACTFL. (1996). Standards for foreign language learning: preparing for the 21st century. https://www.actfl.org/sites/default/files/publications/standards/1996%20National%20Standards%20for%20FL%20L%20Exec%20Summary.pdf

ACTFL. (2015). World-readiness standards for language learning summary. https://www.actfl.org/sites/default/files/publications/standards/World-ReadinessStandardsforLearning Languages.pdf

Allen, H. W. (2010). Language-learning motivation during short-term study abroad: an Activity Theory perspective. *Foreign Language Annals, 43*(1), 27-49. https://doi.org/10.1111/j.1944-9720.2010.01058.x

Anderson, P. H., Hubbard, A., & Lawton, L. (2015). Student motivation to study abroad and their intercultural development. *Frontiers: The Interdisciplinary Journal of Study Abroad, XXVI*, 39-52.

Anderson, P. H., & Lawton, L. (2011). Intercultural development: study abroad vs. on-campus study. *Frontiers: The Interdisciplinary Journal of Study Abroad, XXI*, 86-108.

Bennett, M. (1993). Towards ethnorelativism: a developmental model of intercultural sensitivity. In R. M. Paige (Ed.), *Education for the intercultural experience* (pp. 21-71). Intercultural Press.

Bennett, J. M., & Bennett, M. J. (2004). Developing intercultural sensitivity: an integrative approach to global and domestic diversity. In D. Landis, J. M. Bennett & M. J. Bennett (Eds), *Handbook of intercultural training* (pp. 147-165). Sage. https://doi.org/10.4135/9781452231129.n6

Bohinski, C. A., & Leventhal, Y. (2015). Rethinking the ICC framework: transformation and telecollaboration. *Foreign Language Annals, 48*(3), 521-534. https://doi.org/10.1111/flan.12149

Braskamp, L. A., Braskamp, D. C., & Merrill, K. C. (2009). Assessing progress in intercultural learning and development of students with education abroad experiences. *Frontiers: The Interdisciplinary Journal of Study Abroad, XVIII*, 101-118.

Brubaker, C. (2007). Six weeks in the Eifel: a case for culture learning during short-term study abroad. *Die Unterrichtspraxis/Teaching German, 40*(2), 118-123. https://doi.org/10.1111/tger.2007.40.2.118

Byram, M. (1997). *Teaching and assessing intercultural communicative competence*. Multilingual Matters.

Castañeda, M. E., & Zirger, M. L. (2011). Making the most of the 'new' study abroad: social capital and the short-term sojourn. *Foreign Language Annals, 44*(3), 544-564. https://doi.org/10.1111/j.1944-9720.2011.01146.x

Chieffo, L., & Griffiths, L. (2004). Large-scale assessment of student attitudes after a short-term study abroad program. *Frontiers: The Interdisciplinary Journal of Study Abroad, X*, 165-177.

Chieffo, L., & Griffiths, L. (2009). Here to stay: increasing acceptance of short-term study abroad programs. In R. Lewin (Ed.), *The handbook of practice and research in study abroad* (pp. 365-380). Routledge.

Czerwionka, L., Artamonova, T., & Barbosa, M. (2014). Intercultural competence during short-term study abroad: a focus on knowledge. *Proceedings of the Intercultural Competence Conference, 3*, 46-77.

Davidson, D. E. (2007). Study abroad and outcomes measurements: the case of Russian. *The Modern Language Journal, 91*(2), 276-280. https://doi.org/10.1111/j.1540-4781.2007.00543_13.x

Deardorff, D. K. (2006). Identification and assessment of intercultural competence as a student outcome of internationalization. *Journal of Studies in International Education, 10*(3), 241-266. https://doi.org/10.1177/1028315306287002

Deardorff, D. K. (2009). Implementing intercultural competence assessment. In D.K. Deardorff (Ed.), *The SAGE handbook of intercultural competence* (pp. 477-491). Sage.

Deardorff, D. K. (2012). Framework: intercultural competence model. In K. Berardo & D. K. Deardorff (Eds), *Building cultural competence: innovative activities and models* (pp. 45-52). Stylus.

Donnelly-Smith, L. (2009). Global learning through short-term study abroad. *Peer Review, 11*(4), 12-15.

Dwyer, M. M., & Peters, C. K. (2004). The benefits of study abroad. *Transitions Abroad, 27*(5), 56-59.

Félix-Brasdefer, C., & Hasler-Barker, M. (2015). Complimenting in Spanish in a short-term study abroad context. *System, 48*, 75-85. https://doi.org/10.1016/j.system.2014.09.006

Franklin, K. (2010). Long-term career impact and professional applicability of the study abroad experience. *Frontiers: The Interdisciplinary Journal of Study Abroad, XIX*, 169-190.

Freed, B. F. (1990). Language learning in a study abroad context: the effects of interactive and non-interactive out-of-class contact on grammatical achievement and oral proficiency. In J. Atlantis (Ed.), *Linguistic, language teaching and language acquisition: the interdependence of theory, practice and research* (pp. 459-477). Georgetown University Press.

Goldoni, F. (2015). Preparing students for studying abroad. *Journal of the Scholarship of Teaching and Learning, 15*(4), 1-20.

Hammer, M. R., Bennett, M. J., & Wiseman, R. (2003). Measuring intercultural sensitivity: the intercultural development inventory. *International Journal of Intercultural Relations, 27*(4), 421-443. https://doi.org/10.1016/S0147-1767(03)00032-4

Hart Research Association. (2010). *Raising the bar: employers' views on college learning in the wake of the economic downturn.* Hart Research Associates. https://www.aacu.org/sites/default/files/files/LEAP/2009_EmployerSurvey.pdf

He, Y., Lundgren, K., & Pynes, P. (2017). Impact of short-term study abroad program: inservice teachers' development of intercultural competence and pedagogical beliefs. *Teaching and Teacher Education, 66*(1), 147-157. https://doi.org/10.1016/j.tate.2017.04.012

Ingram, M. (2005). Recasting the foreign language requirement through study abroad: a cultural immersion program in Avignon. *Foreign Language Annals, 38*(2), 211-222. https://doi.org/10.1111/j.1944-9720.2005.tb02486.x

Institute of International Education. (2018). Detailed duration of U.S. study abroad, 2004/05-2016/17. *Open Doors Report on International Educational Exchange.* http://www.iie.org/opendoors

Jackson, J. (2008). *Language, identity and study abroad.* Equinox Publishing.

Jackson, J. (2011). Host language proficiency, intercultural sensitivity, and study abroad. *Frontiers: The Interdisciplinary Journal of Study Abroad, XXI*, 167-188.

Kahn, H. E., & Agnew, M. (2017). Global learning through difference. *Journal of Studies in International Education, 21*(1) 52-64. https://doi.org/10.1177/1028315315622022

Kartoshkina, Y., Chieffo, L., & Kang, T. (2013). Using an internally developed tool to assess intercultural competence in short-term study abroad programs. *International Research and Review: Journal of Phi Beta Delta Honor Society for International Scholars, 3*(1), 23-27.

Kumaravadivelu, B. (2008). *Cultural globalization and language education.* Yale University Press.

Lenkaitis, Calo, S., & Venegas-Escobar, S. (2019). Exploring the intersection of language and culture via telecollaboration: utilizing Zoom for intercultural competence development. *International Multilingual Research Journal.* https://doi.org/10.1080/19313152.2019.1570772

Levine, K. J., & Garland, M. E. (2015). Summer study-abroad program as experiential learning: examining similarities and differences in international communication. *Journal of International Students, 5*(2), 175-187.

Lewis, T. L., & Niesenbaum, R. A. (2005). Extending the stay: using community-based research and service learning to enhance short-term study abroad. *Journal of Studies in International Education, 9*(3), 251-264. https://doi.org/10.1177/1028315305277682

Merriam, S. B. (1998). *Qualitative research and case study applications in education.* Jossey-Bass.

Moeller, A. K., & Nugent, K. (2014). Building intercultural competence in the language classroom. In S. Dhonau (Ed.), *Unlock the gateway to communication* (pp. 1-18). Crown Prints.

NAFSA. (2003). *Securing America's future: global education for a global age. Report of the strategic task force on education abroad.* Association of International Educators. http://www.nafsa.org/Policy_and_Advocacy/Policy_Resources/Policy_Reports/Securing_America_s_Future/

NAFSA. (2019). *Trends in U.S. study abroad.* Association of International Educators. http://www.NAFSA.org

O'Rourke, K. H., & Williamson, J. G. (2002). When did globalisation begin? *European Review of Economic History, 6*(1), 23-50. https://doi-org.libproxy.temple.edu/10.1017/S1361491602000023

Savage, B. L., & Hughes, H. Z. (2014). How does short-term foreign language immersion stimulate language learning? *Frontiers: The Interdisciplinary Journal of Study Abroad, XXIV*, 103-120.

Schulz, R. A. (2007). The challenge of assessing cultural understanding in the context of foreign language instruction. *Foreign Language Annals, 40*(1), 9-26. https://doi.org/10.1111/j.1944-9720.2007.tb02851.x

Serrano, R., Llanes, A., & Tragant, E. (2016). Examining L2 development in two short-term intensive programs for teenagers: study abroad vs. "at home". *System, 57*, 43-54. https://doi.org/10.1016/j.system.2016.01.003

Shiri, S. (2015). Intercultural communicative competence development during and after language study abroad: insights from Arabic. *Foreign Language Annals, 48*(4), 541-569. https://doi.org/10.1111/flan.12162

Shively, R. L. (2015). Developing interactional competence during study abroad: listener responses in L2 Spanish. *System, 48*, 86-98. https://doi.org/10.1016/j.system.2014.09.007

Stebleton, M., Soria, K., & Cherney, B. (2012-2013). The high impact of education abroad: college students' engagement in international experiences and the development of intercultural competencies. *Frontiers: The Interdisciplinary Journal of Study Abroad, XXII*, 1-24.

Stemler, S. E., Imada, T., & Sorkin, C. (2014). Development and validation of the Wesleyan Intercultural Competence Scale (WICS). *Frontiers: The Interdisciplinary Journal of Study Abroad, XXIV*, 25-47.

Tomaš, Z., Farrelly, R., & Haslam, M. (2008). Designing and implementing the TESOL teaching practicum abroad: focus on interaction. *TESOL Quarterly, 42*(4), 660-664. https://doi.org/10.1002/j.1545-7249.2008.tb00155.x

Wang, C. (2010). Toward a second language socialization perspective: issues in study abroad research. *Foreign Language Annals, 43*(1), 50-63. https://doi.org/10.1111/j.1944-9720.2010.01059.x

Williams, T. R. (2009). The reflective model of intercultural competency: a multidimensional, qualitative approach to study abroad assessment. *Frontiers: The Interdisciplinary Journal of Study Abroad, XVIII*, 289-306.

Author index

H
Hilliker, Shannon M. vi, 2, 53
Hüttner, Julia vi, 2, 5

I
Ito, Kinji vi, 2, 53

K
Kodura, Małgorzata vi, 3, 75
Kořínková, Jana vii, 3, 95

L
Lenkaitis, Chesla Ann vii, 3, 137
Lewandowska, Elwira vii, 2, 27
Loranc-Paszylk, Barbara v, 1

M
Marzec-Stawiarska, Małgorzata vii, 3, 115

V
Válková, Silvie vii, 3, 95

www.ingramcontent.com/pod-product-compliance
Lightning Source LLC
Chambersburg PA
CBHW021844220426
43663CB00005B/392